To:

From:

Library of Congress Cataloging-in-Publication Data
Yoder, Harvey, 1939-
Lasting marriage : the owners' manual / Harvey Yoder ; illustrations by Lee E. Eshleman; foreword by John M. Drescher.
p. cm.
Includes bibliographical references.
ISBN 978-0-8361-9354-1 (pbk.)
1. Spouses—Religious life. 2. Marriage—Religious aspects—Christianity. I. Title.
BV4596.M3Y63 2007
248.8'44—dc22
2006100257

Library of Congress Catalog Card Number: 2006100257
International Standard Book Number: 978-0-8361-9354-1
Printed in the United States of America
Book designed by Gwen Stamm
Cover design by Gwen Stamm and Lee Eshleman

14 13 12 11 10 09 08 07 10 9 8 7 6 5 4 3 2 1

To order or request information, please call 1-800-245-7894, or visit www.heraldpress.com.

LASTING MARRIAGE

LASTING MARRIAGE

the *owners' manual*

Harvey Yoder

Illustrations by Lee E. Eshleman
Foreword by John M. Drescher

Herald Press
Scottdale, Pennsylvania
Waterloo, Ontario

Contents

Part II: Basic Marriage Maintenance

Part III: Maintenance Through the Minivan Years

Acknowledgments

Special, special thanks to . . .

Alma Jean, my long-suffering wife, who in spite of knowing all my marital and other flaws, was my most faithful encourager as I wrote this book.

Our three grown children and more recently our grandchildren, each a source of untold inspiration.

The kind folks at Zion Mennonite Church, where I served as pastor for twenty years while also teaching family living and other courses at Eastern Mennonite High School.

The staff and board of the Family Life Resource Center, who have given me many opportunities to grow as a pastor and counselor over the past eighteen years.

Mentors like John Drescher, Paul Schrock, Eugene Souder, Melodie Davis, and many others who have encouraged and helped me in my writing.

The members of Family of Hope House Church, my congregational family and loyal prayer partners.

God, the source of all my blessings, to whom I owe everything.

Foreword

If a car manufacturer had even one out of every hundred vehicles break down completely in the first year or two, imagine the research and study that would go into finding out the reasons why. And how quickly such manufacturers would send out bulletins to deal with the problem!

In the area of marriage, we face a situation that is far more serious. Marriages are breaking up with distressing frequency, but little careful study has been done to examine the causes of such catastrophes. Often more time and effort is spent preparing to walk down the aisle than to walk through the rest of life together.

Harvey Yoder's book for marriage preparation and maintenance can help both those planning to be married and those already married. It provides a combination of short reflections and practical counsel that will benefit couples at any stage of their relationship, as well as point out personal habits and traits that can weaken or strengthen the union. It offers down-to-earth guidance for couples who ask, "Do we have enough going for us to marry?" and to couples who, at some time or another, struggle to stay together.

Yoder realizes that even happy, successful couples have plenty of "irreconcilable differences." But when they divorce and switch to new partners, they gain only a new set of problems, and they often have children who suffer severely.

Surely something is askew when 60 percent of those who divorce and remarry will divorce again, and if children are involved, 75 percent will divorce a second time. According to many studies, few of those who divorce and remarry end up feeling they have actually bettered themselves.

Another important and often overlooked aspect stressed in this book is that of a faith family. Scripture is clear that we can comprehend God's will and blessing only with the help of other Christians. We are not created to go it alone.

My prayer is that *Lasting Marriage: The Owners' Manual* will find acceptance and usefulness in the preparation and maintenance of many a marriage.

—John M. Drescher

Introduction

Some Operating Instructions

It was Valentine's Day 1964. The engagement announcements Alma Jean and I sent to our friends featured a pair of overlapping hearts and the following lines:

two hearts
warmed by breath of God's own love
have met to melt into one

A nice sentiment, but did we really understand what we were saying? And how was it possible (if even desirable) for two hearts to "melt into one"?

No one provided us with an owners' manual to show us how to keep our marriage, like a dependable vehicle, well maintained and running smoothly. Looking back, we could have used large doses of down-to-earth guidance for our marital venture, such as specific help from the Bible, along with other time-tested rules of the road.

Several months before our wedding, we bought our first car together, a slightly used Volkswagen. It too came without a manual, but the former owner helped us with basic operating instructions, and we managed to keep our air-cooled Bug functioning and accident-free until finally its death did us part.

It was years later that I began thinking about creating an owners' manual for the care and maintenance of a marriage. Marriage is, after all, a conveyance meant to last as long as we live, a kind of vehicle God has designed to take us over rough terrain and through a lifetime of hoped-for happiness.

Just how does this marital marvel work? What are the controls by which we safely start it, steer it, control its pace, and above all, avoid a fatal crash?

This book isn't about easy answers for avoiding a relationship breakdown or keeping a marriage from spinning out of control. But I hope some of the things that have helped me and Alma Jean—and many others we know who enjoy a lasting and satisfying relationship—can encourage you on your journey of a lifetime.

Before we start, though, let me note that marriage may not be the best or only choice for everyone. Jesus was successfully and joyfully single, and many of his followers have demonstrated the virtues of living a celibate life. I've even come to believe that learning to first become a satisfied single is one of the best ways to prepare for being successfully married; that whatever qualities help us become content and happy in a single state are the very qualities we need for a good wedded life. But whether married or single, we always need huge amounts of God-empowered self-discipline.

To experience this, let's note the following basic controls:

1. *Our higher brain.* The best marital decisions and behaviors come from the neocortex, the mature, thinking part of our brain. When we allow our lower brain, the impulsive and reactive subcortex, to dominate our actions, our relationships are in serious trouble. Not that this more impulsive and adrenalin-driven part is all bad. In a real emergency, the fight-or-flight arousal it produces can be a great asset. But most of our day-to-day marital problems are best addressed from our cerebral brain, operating under the influence of God's Spirit.

2. *Our Higher Power (God).* Our Creator can best help us keep these amazing brains of ours under good management. God's Word can inform and renew our minds, and God's Spirit can transform and guide our behaviors, enabling us to become the gracious partners God wants us to be.

3. *Our spiritual family.* A community of fellow believers is an invaluable source of control and direction. Just as Scripture declares that it is not good for anyone to be alone, it is also unwise for couples to live without the nurture and guidance of extended families and congregational families.

4. *The Bible, our basic textbook on marriage relationships.* In appendix A, you will find a list of key scriptural themes basic to the care and maintenance of a Christian marriage (these texts on marriage can also be downloaded at www.flrc.org/lastingmarriage.htm). We need to review and apply such wisdom on a regular basis.

So here are four basic controls: our good minds, our great God, our caring congregations, and our trusted road map—the Bible. Now let's look at specific aspects of marriage preparation and maintenance that can help ensure a safe journey to "happily ever after."

Lower-brain-dominated thinking

I'll die if I don't have him/her!

If he/she ever lets me down, it will be terrible!

Alarm! Another problem! It's sure to be a terrible disaster!

I feel so anxious! So angry! So desperate!

Higher-brain-dominated thinking

A good relationship is a gift, one to be treasured for life.

We accept each other as we are—precious but imperfect.

Our problems are just that: problems. With some help, we can learn to handle them.

We can remain calm, confident and peaceful most of the time.

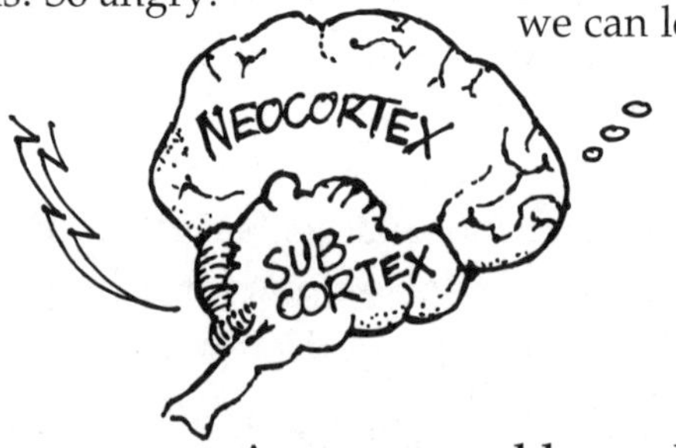

An upper and lower brain scan

Part I
New Owner Preparation

You always marry
the wrong person
You didn't really know
what you thought you knew
when you did what you did
and said what you said.
You didn't know what you needed
or what you needed to know
to choose what you chose
so you can't see what you saw.

You always marry
the right person
Although you really didn't know
what you thought you knew,
you really did know
what you needed to know
when you did what you did.
You knew more than you knew,
you did better than you would
had you known what you didn't.[1]

—David W. Augsburger

1

Rearview Mirror

Look Back Before Moving Forward

The more we acquaint ourselves with our families of origin, the better we're able to understand ourselves and our partner.

In all my years of working with couples in distress, I have seldom met partners who actually lie awake at night thinking up ways to annoy each other. In fact, I've come to believe that most of our behaviors, both the distressing and the helpful ones, result from our simply repeating learned patterns from our past. Too often we find ourselves talking and acting by rote, reacting from habit. And our habits, good and bad, are largely learned from the subculture that is our family of origin.

As a requirement for a marriage and family course Alma Jean and I took some years ago, we researched our family stories as a way of helping us better understand our well-rehearsed ways of thinking and behaving. It was one of our more eye-opening experiences, one we wished we'd had earlier in our relationship. We not only needed a clear windshield for looking forward, but a good rearview mirror to help us reflect on the families that had so shaped us in the early years of our life journeys.

What we've discovered is that the more we acquaint ourselves with our past, the better we understand ourselves and each other. For example, from my very frugal farm family I learned to be mildly obsessive about conserving things like food, energy, and of course, money, which was always in short supply. So among my internal rules were "Keep the showers short," "Turn off all lights when not in use," "Never throw away anything you might use sometime." Alma Jean's family was also financially stressed, but her schoolteacher father was at least a little better off, and she turned out to be a little less stingy than I.

With this awareness of our differences, we needed to find some middle ground in working out disagreements over money and to learn to remain calm in the process. We had to remind ourselves that such conflicts didn't have to be huge crises, but they were ordinary difficulties like those experienced by most couples, and caring people like ourselves could learn to work them out.

That's a major theme in this book: learning to fully accept and respect each other, differences and all. If we are too quick to take offense or to accuse our spouse of intentionally distressing us, we become highly anxious and upset, and can create mountains out of the smallest molehills. That has happened all too often in our marriage, when in a desperate attempt to fix things, we resorted to strategies that only made things worse and to unhelpful patterns of behavior we had learned in our families of origin.

Our nearly two years of dating and engagement would have been great times to learn more about each other's family scripts and stories, behaviors and attitudes. We could have begun earlier the good work of better understanding our interactions as a couple and more fully appreciating the strengths we brought into our relationship.

Here are two reflections on my own family stories. They are meant to encourage you and your partner to ponder your own. I begin with my father's.

Blessed by My Yoder Roots

I don't cry easily, but I couldn't help losing it during the forty-five-minute ride home from the last night I spent with my eighty-year-old father, Ben, who was dying of emphysema. Not only was I grieving the loss of my one and only Dad—gentle and generous to a fault—I was also mourning the father with whom I had never fully connected.

Financial struggles our family went through as I was growing up limited my father's energy and time for his nine children. It was on that long ride home that I realized how much I still wished for more memories of things like fishing, playing ball, or going for walks with Dad and of sharing with him more of my dreams and innermost feelings.

Yet I was also aware of how much more he had given me than he had ever received as a child. My father lost his mother when he was three, and that was my grandfather Dan's third experience of being a widower. His first wife had died of measles at twenty-three, leaving him with a two-year-old son and a nine-month-old daughter, who died the day of her mother's funeral. A decade later Dan's second wife died of tuberculosis at twenty-nine, leaving him with five more children to care for. Two years later, Dan married Elizabeth, my grandmother, and had another daughter and two more sons, the youngest of whom was Ben, my father. Then at thirty-five, when Dad was three, Elizabeth died of complications from her fourth pregnancy, leaving my grandfather, at forty-four, with nine living children.

My father didn't remember much of his next five years except of sometimes crying at night wishing he had a mother like other children did. He also wished for a warmer, more nurturing father instead of one he described as a "man of sorrows."

When my father was eight, Dan married a widow with a number of children and stepchildren of her own. While Dad was glad to have a real mother again (and some new siblings to play with) the families didn't blend well, and the rest of my father's childhood was marked by constant tension and distress.

I've sometimes wondered what kind of parent would ordinarily come out of this troubled, *mis*functional family. Remarkably, instead of becoming a depressed or angry man, Dad was one of the kindest and most gracious human beings I've ever known—even though he had never learned how to really hug us as children or to lavish us with praise. (We did teach him to hug in his later years, though!)

On his deathbed, my father breathed the words of his favorite song, "Blessed Assurance," the title of which appears on his tombstone. He had learned to live a new life and celebrate a new lyric, "This is my story, this is my song, praising my Savior all the day long."

I often wish I could tell my father once again how blessed I feel for the way he turned his grief into an amazing grace.

I'm Blessed to Be a Nisly Too (and a Troyer, Miller, Hochstetler, et cetera)

My mother, Mary Nisly, was child number nine in a family of thirteen; I was number eight in a family of nine. She grew up in the home with a father and mother whose simple faith was an integral part of their lives; I was blessed with equally devout parents. She enjoyed reading, entertaining, gardening, and traveling; so do I. My mother was a keen judge of human nature, could recognize her own flaws and those of others, and had a certain and clear sense of what was right and wrong, good and bad. Sometimes, like her, I am too critical of myself and others, too intolerant of those with whom I differ.

A plucky half-pint of a woman, my mom died of cancer at sixty-seven. On her gravestone is the title of one of her favorite gospel songs, "I need no mansion here below." Her childhood home was certainly no mansion, and she died in the modest mobile home my parents bought for their retirement. Frugal to a fault, she knew how to make her life rich in a multitude of ways, by her love of gardening, by growing flowers and raising canaries, by her enjoyment of music and books, and by her gracious hospitality and many friends. As a child I was blessed by her hugs and by the example of her quiet faith in God and her service to others.

My parents were far from perfect, and they experienced their share of depressed and distressed moods. They were far too conflict-avoidant and overstressed the need for everyone to be nice at all costs, even if it meant sweeping important issues under the rug. But each was a far better parent than I could have ever deserved.

I hope that somehow my folks, and Alma Jean's, are still aware of the large debt we will forever owe them. They gave us our life and, for better or worse, have powerfully shaped our life direction. Remembering their contributions reminds us of other members of our families and of the many friends with whom we need to stay more up-to-date in the appreciation department.

In summary, there is probably no better place to start preparing for a good future than to take stock of our past. That past is always present, always a significant part of our continued story.

See the family of origin inventory in appendix B.

For more information about family of origin issues, visit www.marriagepreparation.org/FamOrigHoxey.htm.

2

A Thorough Inspection

Pursue Personal Growth to Become a Better Partner

Before we join someone in marriage, we'd better make sure we have a good supply of personal happiness to bring with us.

A common myth about marriage is that it can transform an unhappy person into a happy and healthy one. The truth is that if we choose to join ourselves to someone for life, we'd better bring an abundant supply of happiness and healthiness with us. Of course, in a good marriage we can share and multiply our joy, but being a married couple will never automatically produce it. If we come together with our emotional fuel tank near empty and with the expectation that our spouse should be able to fill it, we are setting ourselves up for major resentment and disappointment.

Likewise, if we suffer from emotional problems like chronic depression or anxiety, it is critically important to seek whatever help we need to make sure we will be able to experience reasonably good mental health throughout our married years. Our partner can be our best friend, but we should never expect him or her to be our therapist.

So a formula for a happily-ever-after relationship might be something like this: (1) Take responsibility for your own emotional and spiritual health in order to become a better *person.* (2) Become a better *person* in order to be a better *partner.* (3) Practice being a good *partner* in preparation for being a more effective *parent.*

It all starts with the hard work of being a genuinely good man or woman. The following reflections may help you develop your own vision of what a healthy, whole person and partner should be like.

Being a Good Man

Macho. Crude. Insensitive. Controlling. Obsessed with sex. These are some typical stereotypes our society has of men.

Most of us agree these labels aren't true of all males all the time, but we know far too many who leer at women, demean them by focusing on their body parts, and at times use, abuse, and abandon them. Sometimes men are anything but good people.

I'll never forget the advice an older teacher once gave: "If you want a good woman, you have to be a good man. It's as simple as that."

That's pretty basic. Just be a good man. You deserve only the kind of person you are. But what is that kind of person like? Here are some ideas for starters:

- A good man shows a high level of respect for everyone. He treats women the way he would have other men treat his own daughter, mother, or sister.
- A good man strives to be a good lover, but realizes love has more to do with being patient than with being passionate, with being kind and dependable than with being amorous in bed.
- A good man is honest. An "I love you" is never used just to get someone to give him what he wants, but is matched by kind, caring behavior in every part of his life.
- A good man doesn't indulge in pornographic fantasies of artificially endowed models dying to have sex with him. He recognizes pornography as not only infantile but also dangerously addictive and downright harmful to relationships.
- A good man honors his commitments. When he says "for better or for worse," he means it. When he promises "until death do us part," he honors that promise.
- A good man knows how to be a decent dad. He takes a strong interest in his children and provides for their physical, emotional, and spiritual needs. They are always a major priority in his life.

Is being this kind of good man really possible? Not perfectly, of course, but it's what God created each of us to be and what God can enable each of us to become.

The Bible tells the story of David, who when he had committed adultery and then realized the awfulness of what he had done, cried out to God in one of the greatest prayers of repentance in the Bible—Psalm 51. God honored him by calling him a man after God's own heart. Likewise, God will love and bless those who pursue becoming good men, regardless of their past.

Such men are more likely to find a good woman—not a perfect one, but one more like the amazing spouse described in Proverbs 31:10-12:

> A wife of noble character who can find?
> She is worth far more than rubies.
> Her husband has full confidence in her
> and lacks nothing of value.
> She brings him good, not harm,
> all the days of her life.

Being a Good Woman

> She speaks with wisdom,
> and faithful instruction is on her tongue.
> She watches over the affairs of her household
> and does not eat the bread of idleness.
> Her children arise and call her blessed;
> her husband also, and he praises her:
> "Many women do noble things,
> but you surpass them all." (31:26-29)

This description of a "wife of noble character" may seem like an impossible ideal, but it is also refreshingly different from images of women common today. This good woman is not defined primarily by her marital or maternal role but is portrayed as an entrepreneur, a manager, a craftsperson, a merchandiser. She has a full and purpose-driven life.

There are no two females (or males) alike, of course. Each has a unique set of strengths and gifts. I feel especially blessed by the strengths of good women in my life—my mother, my wife, and my daughter, in my opinion, being among the finest!

Here are some of the qualities of women I most admire:

- A good woman shows a high level of respect for herself, with an equal respect for others around her. She recognizes that healthy self-respect is sometimes difficult because of negative inner voices from her past.
- A good woman combines toughness with tenderness, a healthy assertiveness with a gracious spirit and a warm heart. She realizes that having the courage to do this isn't always easy if she has been conditioned only to be "nice" and never make waves.
- A good woman is straightforward in expressing her needs and feelings. She doesn't expect others she loves to be able to read her mind but is able to speak her own mind in clear and respectful ways.
- A good woman celebrates and takes good care of the beautiful body God gave her. She neither publicly flaunts it nor tries to imitate media and market-driven images of young, airbrushed models and celebrities. Her beauty radiates from deep inside and fully reflects God's image and presence in her life.
- A good woman is faithful to the core—to God, to her family, and to her church family—but not solely out of a sense of obliga-

tion or martyr-like duty. She is also joyful and faithful in the use of her varied gifts, always for God's glory and the good of others.

- A good woman is capable of being a dedicated mom. She sets a strong example as a parent who is devoted to her children and committed to helping them grow to become good women and men of God.

Charm is deceptive, and beauty is fleeting;
but a woman who fears the Lord is to be praised.
Give her the reward she has earned,
and let her works bring her praise at the city gate. (31:30-31)

Does all this sound hard? Of course it does, but that's where our faith can help empower each of us to become all we can be. Who would want to be anything less?

An inventory of good personal and marital qualities can be found in appendixes C and H.

3

Before You Say, 'I Might'

Choose Carefully to Avoid Regrets

*By the time most couples come for premarital counseling,
it's usually too late to deal with the most basic question,
Should we get married at all?*

I had many opportunities to do premarital counseling in my twenty years as pastor of a two-hundred-member congregation and a part-time teacher of family life courses at Eastern Mennonite High School in Harrisonburg, Virginia. What often struck me during that counseling was that, by the time most couples came for their first session, it was too late to be asking the most important question: whether it was wise for them to get married at all. Usually their wedding date had already been set, and the couple was well on their way to the altar.

So I began encouraging those in dating relationships to arrange for *pre-engagement* counseling, or at least to talk things over with a pastor or other counselor before actually announcing their engagement. The idea spread, and numerous couples began to ask for such sessions.

Later, as a part-time counselor at Eastern Mennonite University (EMU), I introduced an annual workshop called "To Knot or Not to Knot?" for seriously dating but not-yet-engaged couples. This three-hour session began with a discussion panel of a recently married couple, an older couple, and a divorced person, each honestly sharing what they had learned from their own relationship. The female attendees then met for questions and conversation with the women presenters and the males with the male panelists. Each couple then completed a discussion exercise using sample questions from a premarital inventory.

A special focus of the workshop was distinguishing between normal differences and polar opposites. Most people agree that opposites do attract. For example, we may be drawn to someone who is compulsively neat and well organized as a way of making up for our lack of order and structure, while our partner may feel drawn to our more laid-back and spontaneous approach to life (but all the while assuming we will someday become more like them, that is, change for the better!). In real life, though, any opposite traits are sure to cause major frustrations. This is especially true if our extreme differences involve matters of faith and values.

Another example of differences that can make things worse over time is the tendency of one person to be a maximizer (making a big issue of things) while the other is a minimizer. In this kind of relationship, the more one partner maximizes, the more the other minimizes, and vice versa. The same dynamic happens when one spouse tends to overfunction (take on more than his or her share of responsibility) and unwittingly adds to the likelihood that the other person will underfunction, and vice versa. These are just a few of the ways opposing traits and tendencies can drive couples further and further apart.

Not surprisingly, some of the folks involved in the above pre-engagement workshops or counseling sessions ended their relationships. This was usually because one or both were already having serious reservations and needed help either to work through some major conflicts or to end the relationship. Neither is ever a happy prospect, but either is still far better than having a major disruption or a divorce later.

Will pre-engagement and premarital counseling guarantee that every couple will enjoy a happy, lifelong marriage? Hardly. But if it helps even a few couples avoid the heartbreak of a later divorce and establish more stable marriage and family relationships, it is certainly worth the effort.

Another brain scan:

Lower-brain-dominated thinking	*Higher-brain-dominated thinking*
I want all of him/her—now.	I'd rather take plenty of time than have tons of regret.
I will do anything to get the mate I want.	I want a mutual friend, not a conquest.
I don't care what misgivings other people have about my future mate.	I welcome other people's perspectives about our relationship.
Physical attractiveness, money, and popularity are all-important.	Good personal qualities and values are what matter most.

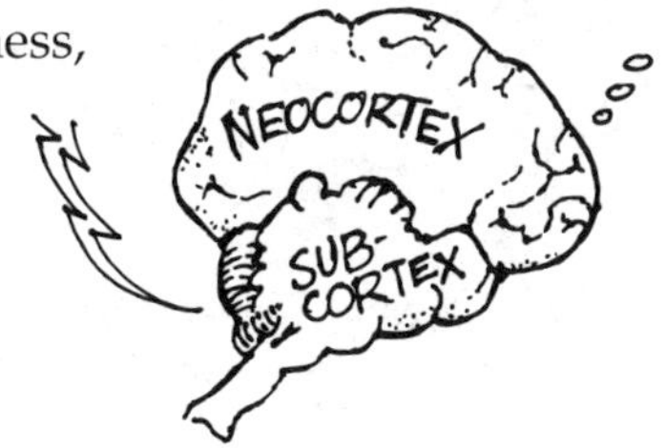

See appendix D for printable copies of some questions from the "To Knot or Not to Knot?" workshop, and appendix K for a prenuptial covenant for engaged couples.

When Daniel O'Brien-Richards-Montague-Wilson gave his engagement gift to Janice Strite-Jones-Ross-Hershberger...

4

A Celebration for the Truly Rich

Start with a Well-Planned Wedding

Christian weddings need to represent a different kind of wealth, a celebration of all that is truly beautiful and enduring in our lives.

Alma Jean and I have enjoyed being guests at lots of weddings over the years. We usually find them to be carefully rehearsed performances that begin with anxious anticipation and end with a general sense of relief and celebration.

And they often cost a small fortune. But my wife and I attended one some time ago that represented a different kind of wealth. The bride, a family friend, and the bridegroom welcomed each of us as we arrived. He wore a plain white shirt and ordinary dress pants, she a matching white blouse and a dark skirt. There was no formal processional, no elaborately decorated chapel, not even the traditional bridesmaids and groomsmen. All of us were to be the wedding party and to enjoy the festive atmosphere the couple and their families created for this once-in-a-lifetime celebration.

As we sat down, we noted a cloth-covered table in the front of the chapel with a variety of white candles, a visual feast of light and warmth for the ceremony. Beside it was a live tree from a local nursery to be planted after the reception as a symbol of the couple's new life together. Music was plentiful and wonderful, and included congregational hymns that everyone sang with enthusiasm. Several brief meditations were personally addressed to the young pair seated in the front row. As they stood to pledge their vows to each other and to receive blessings offered by friends and family members, many of us were moved to tears.

At the reception there was plenty of hot cider and two kinds of soup for the guests, followed by a generous slice of zucchini cake, all of which had been prepared by various friends of the bride and groom. After the meal, a time of reminiscing and story telling helped us to get better acquainted with the couple and to learn more about their after-honeymoon plans: she to take a volunteer service assignment and he to enter graduate school.

I don't know how much this wedding cost, but with no pearl-studded gowns or rented tuxedos, no caterers or lavish floral arrangements, no stretch limousines or silver candelabras, it was considerably less than the national average of around twenty thousand dollars. Yet there was something about the service that seemed especially rich and elegant. It was less a staged performance than a time of community togetherness, one in which we felt a close connection both with the couple and with the God who smiled a warm blessing on the whole affair.

It makes me wonder whether we shouldn't encourage investing more of our resources in helping couples prepare for a lasting *marriage* and less in exhaustive preparations for a thirty-minute display of wealth out of keeping with our Christian values. Really great weddings should represent a different kind of abundance, a celebration of all that is truly beautiful and enduring in our lives.

Our singer-songwriter son wrote the following piece for his younger brother's and his younger sister's weddings, both held in the fall of 2001. The song expresses some of the mystery and blessing of two of our family's most unforgettable experiences.

Wedding Song
the ones you love all gathered 'round
to bless the day, the love you've found,
with song and prayer and a joyful sound,
it's good to be together.

as you were loved when you were small,
so may you grow, then, when you fall
you'll get back up and shake it off,
and travel on together.

a mystery to see you through,
how 1 and 1 is more than 2,
a cord of 3 strands binding you, and
it's not easily broken.

the simplest magic known to us:
to come to care, to learn to trust,
to love what's there at any cost,
to learn to be together.[2]
—*Brad K. Yoder*

See appendix E for some ideas for wedding planning.

When an optimist and a pessimist marry.

For additional ideas for planning simple and creative weddings, check www.simpleliving.org for information about The Alternative Wedding Book.

5

Making the Payments

Budget for Just and Joyful Living

Love is blind, but when it comes to money,
marriage is the greatest eye opener of them all.

In Leonard Bernstein's musical *Candide*, two lovers share their dreams of a wonderful future together. The future groom sings the praises of becoming a simple farmer with a garden and some cows and chickens. The bride-to-be responds with her dream of owning fine jewelry, being world travelers, and doing lots of elaborate entertaining. They then exuberantly conclude with the duet, "Oh happy pair. Oh happy we! It's very rare how we agree!"

Indeed, love can be blissfully blind, but marriage is the greatest eye opener imaginable. And in no area is this more so than in our finances.

When you think about it, it is our day-to-day spending that most accurately reflects our real values. That is, whenever we invest in something, we are literally showing how much value we place on that particular product or service. Of course, no two people's values are exactly the same. And since we will always have a limited sum of money, we soon realize that whatever our partner spends may keep us from getting some of the things *we* want. Thus the compromises we need to make about money are never easy.

What makes this even harder is that many of us think of finances as a very private matter, details of which we seldom share with even our closest friends. Add to this the fact that we are constantly bombarded with media messages urging us to spend more than we have on things we really don't need, and it's easy to see how often money matters result in major marital conflicts.

As followers of Jesus, we are called not only to provide for each other but also to share generously with those in need. Jesus promises we will be most blessed, most happy, when we put God's rule ("kingdom") and God's rules ("righteousness") first. Then we can celebrate a truly anxiety-free and joy-filled life.

The following are some practical tips on how to live more simply and more justly:

- Make generous giving a top budget priority. You will feel richer and better about yourselves and learn valuable self-discipline in the process.
- Avoid buying new vehicles, and keep the one(s) you own now for at least ten years or well over 100,000 miles (unless you are paying too much for one you can't afford).
- As much as possible, avoid borrowing for anything that you consume or that depreciates in value. Use credit cards only for short-term emergencies and for amounts that can be paid before interest accrues.

- Plant your own garden for great food and good exercise. Use available mulch to save moisture, cut down on weeding, and lessen the need for a tiller.
- Reduce exposure to TV and other media ads, and talk back to or ignore the misleading ads you do see and hear.
- Refuse to buy even bargains on impulse, but shop from prepared lists.
- Avoid super-sized homes that require a mint in interest, maintenance, and utility costs.
- Share lawn mowers, tillers, pickups, and more expensive tools and other items with good friends, neighbors, or family members.
- Normally avoid brand-name clothing and food items in favor of store brands and buying at thrift shops.
- Reduce purchases of soft drinks, snack foods, and over-packaged and overpriced convenience foods.
- Get insurance coverage only for losses you wouldn't be able to cover from your savings or other accounts. Combining several kinds of insurance with the same company can also save you money.
- Reduce, reuse, and recycle in whatever ways possible.

To be successful and faithful in managing your resources, you may want to enlist the help of a trusted financial mentor or couple. Prudent planning can go a long way in keeping financial problems from dominating and distressing a relationship.

See appendix F for more on Jesus' teachings about money.

For more resources to help in your budget planning, visit www.mma-online.org and www.crown.org/tools/budgetguide.asp.

6

The Best for Last

Save Sexual Intimacy for Marriage —Then Celebrate It for Life

Sexual intercourse has an unforgettably bonding effect, capable of creating a sense of oneness at least as strong as saying 'I do' three times in a wedding ceremony.

There is one unwritten rule most of us never break: Wait until December 25 to open your Christmas presents. Why? Because we know that the preparation and anticipation involved in our time of waiting will double the pleasure of gift giving and receiving.

That's even truer when it comes to the full enjoyment of one of God's most special gifts, our sexuality. Wise love waits for the wedding night not just because it is a biblical rule but because waiting makes it possible for us to become better prepared and more certain of our choice before we "go all the way." It then allows us to celebrate with sheer joy and abandonment.

Clearly our society urges us to skip the waiting. Instant gratification is the norm in almost every movie love story and is the mindset promoted in countless ads urging us to buy and indulge with no thought for tomorrow. It's easy to see that the very idea of chastity goes against the grain of the throwaway, buy-now-and-pay-later lifestyle on which our consumer economy depends. But the results of applying that kind of self-indulgent, instant gratification thinking to a sexual relationship can range from disappointment to downright despair.

But what if we're already engaged, already pledged to each other?

No matter how committed we may feel, most of us don't think of engagement as the same as being a married couple—and for good reasons. People have been known to break their engagement, as sometimes they should. This arrangement is, after all, intended to be a final test of whether two people are a good match for each other, a time of making sure before the knot is actually tied.

From both a scriptural and an emotional perspective, sexual intercourse has an unforgettably bonding effect, one that powerfully "marries" us to another whether we are ready or not. If we *are* actually ready to experience this kind of superglue bonding with the one we love, why not go ahead with first having the public ceremony, *then* the consummation in bed?

I have often heard people regretting not having become officially married before becoming "one flesh." On the other hand, I know of no couples who waited and later wished they hadn't. Why? Because they found such exquisite pleasure in celebrating their "first time" in a relaxed honeymoon atmosphere, after they had publicly pledged their vows and been officially and lavishly blessed by their families, friends, and congregations. Then they had no anxiety about getting caught or becoming pregnant, fewer feelings of inhibition or anxiety, and no fear of abandonment or guilt afterward. They were truly going "all the way" for life.

So the scriptural direction to first leave father and mother, and "cleave"—that is, commit to—our spouse, *then* to "be one flesh" isn't about our Creator laying down some arbitrary rule (Genesis 2:24 KJV). It's simply a formula that puts first things first. And according to a landmark 1995 study, *Sex in America: a Definitive Survey*, faithful monogamous couples report being significantly more satisfied with the sexual aspects of their lives than those in uncommitted relationships.[3]

God's plan works. The alternative, engaging in sexual intimacy without the safeguard of a marital covenant, is somewhat like starting a fire in one's living room before first building a fireplace with a good flue. Fire is powerful and can provide wonderful warmth and enjoyment, but without a safe structure to contain it, it can also cause untold harm and heartache.

Is there forgiveness for sexual indiscretions, for engaging in some form of "premarital marriage"? Or pardon for couples who have decided to just "live together," something once referred to as "common law *marriage*"? Thankfully, yes. Whenever we confess our mistakes, seek healing for past failures, and get whatever help we need to work through leftover guilt or pain, God is gracious in restoring us and helping us start a new chapter in our lives. With God it's never too late to begin again, to experience a "new birth" in a relationship, even to feel some degree of restored virginity.

Yet, like a loving parent, God wants us to enjoy the very best Christmas possible. That's why we're given this simple rule: Wait until you're wed—then celebrate for a lifetime.

Part II
Basic Marriage Maintenance

Keep in mind that people do not fall out of love
the way they do out of trees. Relationship decline is neither
a sudden nor an inevitable process. When love and happiness
do decline, it usually follows a steady and relentless erosion
of satisfaction due to unbounded and destructive conflict.
Our message is: You can stem the tide of erosion by learning
to handle conflict constructively.

—Clifford Notarious and Howard Markman[4]

7

Introducing the Relationship Maintenance Department

Somehow we've gotten the foolish idea that the longer we're in a relationship, the less care it needs to keep it alive and thriving.

I once heard the story of a pair of newlyweds who were given a new Mercedes-Benz as a wedding gift. They truly loved their car and enjoyed driving it every day. There was only one major problem: neither bothered to check or change the oil.

One fateful day, while the couple was speeding along on a busy interstate, the engine in their beautiful Benz froze up and refused to go any further. Wouldn't budge. The oil in the crankcase had become a grimy, gooey mess, resulting in this once great machine experiencing a sad and untimely death.

Marital moral of the story? Even a Mercedes kind of marriage, one with the most ideally matched pair and picture-perfect wedding, will fail if we don't pay attention to maintenance.

Not unlike this couple with the Mercedes, somehow we've gotten the foolish idea that the longer we're in a relationship, the less care it will need to keep it alive and thriving. We need to reverse that thinking. In fact, every new bride or groom should be given this one clear instruction: *Whatever wonderful and considerate things you did to win your partner's love you should do at least as regularly and just as creatively to keep it alive.*

Here is a sample of some good maintenance activities for couples.

Daily:
(1) A warm, conversational chat of no less than ten minutes.
(2) At least one ten-second hug.
(3) Two or more compliments or I-love-yous.
(4) A prayer time together.

Weekly:
(1) Some kind of date for just the two of you.
(2) A meeting to review your past week and plan your next one.
(3) A love-you note or card.

Monthly:
(1) A really special date or celebration.

Annually:
(1) A weekend honeymoon.
(2) A marriage enrichment seminar, and/or
(3) A checkup of your marital health with a pastor, counselor, or mentor couple.

These kinds of efforts may require a lot of work, but when you think of it, isn't a great marriage worth even more than a good Mercedes? Assuming you agree, you will find this section helpful in introducing four areas in which preventive maintenance can help insure a truly lasting marriage.[5]

Problem-Free Area (PFA)
Maintenance Tasks: We make sure our joint relationship tank remains full by consistently showing respect for each other and arranging for lots of good conversation, work, and play together.

Personal Problem Area (PPA)
Maintenance Tasks: We recognize and take full responsibility for each of our individual issues that call for change and growth, and avoid minimizing personal faults or blaming others for them.

Spouse's Problem Area (SPA)
Maintenance Tasks: We neither rush in to fix nor become judgmental when we recognize a problem in our partner, but practice attentive listening and offer encouragement and support.

Mutual Problem Area (MPA)
Maintenance Tasks: We take turns talking to and listening to each other in this joint area, take time to brainstorm new solutions to mutual problems, and take part in regular negotiation and "couple's meeting" sessions, as well as being willing to get help from a third-party mediator if necessary.

The next four chapters focus on how to keep a marriage well maintained in each of these areas.

For help in identifying and recognizing problem ownership in the above categories, take the pretest in appendix G.

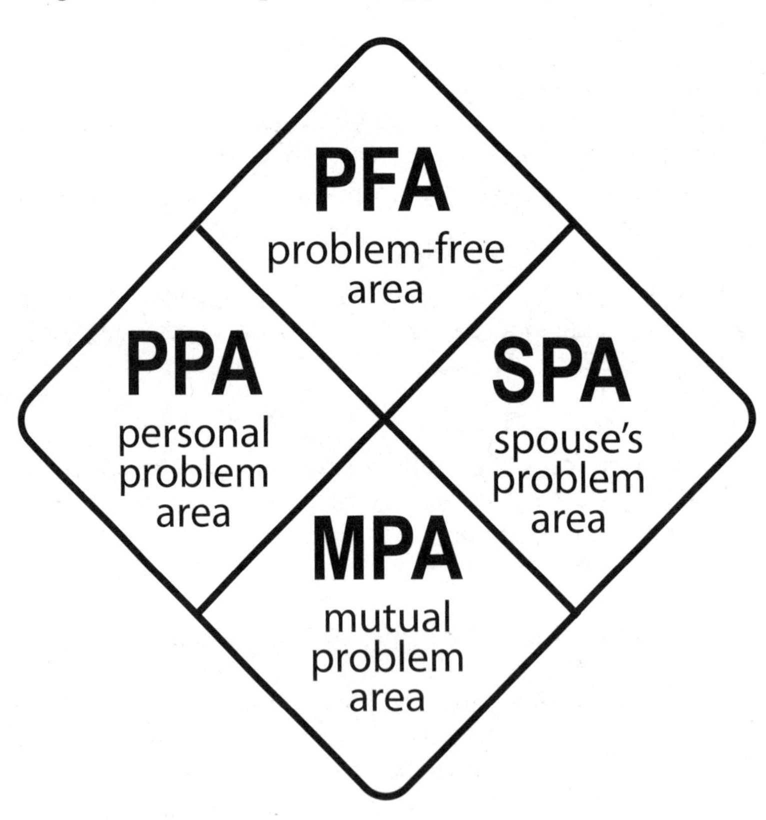

8

Problem-Free Area (PFA)

Take Time to Work, Pray, and Play Together

The more couples work at expanding their Problem-Free Area, the smaller and more manageable their other problem areas become.

Success in marriage is often tied to one simple, well-practiced habit: couples focus more time and energy on conflict-free activities than on their problems and differences. They do not deny or minimize their conflicts, but remain committed to spending 80 percent of their together time in the Problem-Free Area (PFA).

As dating couples and newlyweds we tend to be great in this department. We try hard to be on our best behavior and are likely to freely give our partner the benefit of every doubt. When asked about problems, we may deny having any, or insist that whatever minor ones we have will work themselves out in time. Thus for as long as possible we cling to the dream of becoming the world's first perfect pair.

There is much that's good about that mind-set. It helps us form the kind of strong bond and the reservoir of good feelings we are sure to need later when things get hard. And the more we work at keeping our PFA emotional tank filled, the more that part of our life thrives and the smaller and more manageable our problem areas become.

Of course, it is possible for new lovers to become far too focused on minimizing or dismissing problems. Sooner or later, some issues are sure to beg for attention. But even then we will always need to maintain well-kept problem-free "rooms" in our marital house, living areas we jealously guard from being randomly and routinely invaded by conflicts. For this to happen, each partner must take at least 50 percent of the responsibility for adding to and maintaining the PFA. Meanwhile, each must learn to file away or set aside problems that need to be worked out—but at other times—in the Mutual Problem Area (MPA).

While the PFA may at first seem easiest to maintain, it is also the easiest to neglect. When it is ignored and when normal difficulties do develop, we typically become overanxious and overly focused on our problems. Or when things are going reasonably well, we can be lulled into thinking that everything will take care of itself in this department without us investing the time, energy, and creativity we need to keep our relationship alive and thriving.

In summary, taking this area for granted is a big mistake, but investing lots of time and energy in PFA activities like the following is sure to produce big dividends.

- Offer an affectionate touch as often as possible.
- Take turns initiating daily "mini dates" (short walks, talks or other 10-30 minute activities).
- Write frequent love notes.
- Plan a weekly evening out.
- Practice making at least four positive comments for every one complaint or concern expressed.
- Share household chores.
- Give regular back rubs, foot rubs, or other body massages.
- Attend a marriage seminar or retreat every few years.
- Read something inspirational and pray together every day.
- Develop memorable traditions around special events and dates.
- Repeat and renew marriage vows at every anniversary.
- Enjoy celebrative lovemaking—regularly and passionately—as desired by both.

Speaking of making love, successful couples have learned that one of the most important areas to safeguard from intrusion by problems is their bedroom. While passionate lovemaking isn't the be-all and end-all of married life (most couples spend only a fraction of their total time together at this), the quality of a couple's romantic life is still one of the better indicators of their marital health. If a relationship is going well (and assuming there are no physical or emotional problems that interfere) most spouses will regularly feel physically attracted and downright amorous toward each other. But when resentments and tensions mount, this is often one of the first parts of a relationship to suffer.

This may be especially true for women. While there are exceptions to all generalizations about gender differences, men tend to see sex as a way of resolving tensions, while women may have a greater need to address problems first, then celebrate reconciliation by being intimate. Each perspective is partly right.

Here are some maintenance tips for a problem-free and joy-filled love life:

- Make lovemaking about more than just sex. Think of every act of helpfulness, every kind gesture, every word of appreciation as a form of *pre*-foreplay, a buildup of desire for God-blessed intimacy in bed.
- Be sure to talk about problems in this department at times other than when you're about to make out or to make love. Sexual and other sensitive issues are best talked about in couple's meetings (see chapter 11), not at the times or places where you experience your most intimate moments. So if you need to do any serious negotiation about your lovemaking, you may want to leave your bedroom and go to an agreed-on place elsewhere to talk it out.
- Keep your physical intimacy playful and relaxed. Don't pay too much attention to how-to manuals that portray sexual activity as an athletic performance.
- Remember, most couples don't have simultaneous or multiple orgasms on a regular basis. And what is considered normal for frequency of intercourse varies widely from couple to couple. Sex should be about pleasuring and loving each other, not about assigning grades or keeping score.

- Insist on keeping all thoughts of sexual unfaithfulness, including all forms of pornography, out of your personal and fantasy life. God has given you each other to explore and to savor for life, and it's not necessary to become tired of or bored with each other's bodies and personalities.
- Pay attention to good hygiene and other aspects of your appearance, even in bed (or *especially* in bed). Don't neglect to stroke, touch, caress, and flatter the love of your life as if she or he were the most special person—and you the most devoted lover—in the world.
- Avoid watching TV in your bedroom. According to author Aline Zoldbrod, "Past the falling-in-love stage, sex doesn't just happen unless you make it happen. . . . You can't just coast, you have to steer. And if your TV is in your bedroom, then you coast into watching TV."[6]
- Keep your expectations modest and realistic. Your desire for physical lovemaking may not come at the same time as your partner's and may be more, or less, frequent or intense. This is normal and represents just one of many ways this part of your relationship helps you learn patience and maturity.
- If you need medical or counseling help in this or any other area, don't hesitate to consult a trusted doctor, marital or sex therapist, pastor, or other good mentor. Life is too short not to experience the best of this and every other part of your marriage.
- Refer to and practice the first of the above instructions every day.

Janelle and Rob post a new sign on their bedroom door.

9

Personal Problem Area (PPA)

Take Responsibility for Your Own Behavior and Happiness

Most problems in a marriage aren't actually marital as such, but are the result of personal problems that negatively impact the marriage.

I like the unity candle ritual in marriage ceremonies, when the bride and groom each take a lighted candle and together light a third one symbolizing their union. I am uncomfortable, though, if the individual candles are then extinguished, as though the two were now only a blended "us" and no longer an individual "me" and "you."

Yes, becoming a wedded pair does mean being joined together, united, to form a more perfect union. But a marriage will always be primarily whatever two individuals bring to it. If what we bring is gracious and good, it results in our happiness being multiplied, our lives being enriched and blessed. But if what we bring is rude, irritable, or self-centered, it adds a distress that can also have a multiplying and misery-producing effect.

In my years of counseling couples, I have come to see most problems in a marriage not as *marital* in their origin but as *individual* problems that are having a powerful impact on the marriage. For that reason, getting individual counseling or mentoring can be even more important than just going for marriage counseling when a relationship is in trouble.

My natural tendency is to focus on my spouse's problems. If only she would change, all would be well! But to the extent that I focus on her issues instead of mine, that in itself becomes the problem, since that is where I clearly have the *least* power to bring about any improvement. When I work on me, on that half of the marital equation for which I am responsible, I can begin to make an immediate and positive difference.

I used to think that just going through a wedding ceremony would somehow rid us each of our undesirable traits. Surely my new spouse would become the ideal partner I had always dreamed of, and together we would be transformed into something new, a blended, unselfish pair quite unlike the far-from-perfect individuals we were before. Unfortunately, becoming married doesn't produce such magic. It may, in fact, bring out our worst. If that happens, our good relationship can turn into a nightmare, all because we haven't focused on getting our own bad habits under control.

Is it realistic to expect that we can change our own long-standing patterns—such as negative attitudes, frequent anger outbursts, or general irritability—even if we try hard? Can old dogs learn new tricks or leopards change their spots?

For a start, we are neither dogs nor leopards (though such creatures often demonstrate better behavior than many humans do). And we're not talking about any "tricks" here or any changes in our "spots," as in physical attributes, but about changes in our attitudes and actions. These are all learned patterns of behavior that, with God's help, we can unlearn or replace with new ones.

Rabbi Joseph Telushkin, author of *Words That Hurt, Words That Heal*, sometimes asks people if they think they could go for twenty-four hours without saying an unkind word to or about anyone. Most respond with an instant no. He then says, "All of you who can't answer yes must recognize what a serious problem you have. Because if I asked you to go for twenty-four hours without drinking liquor, and you said, 'I can't do that,' I'd tell you, 'Then you recognize you are an alcoholic.' . . . Similarly, if you can't go for twenty-four hours without saying unkind words . . . then you've lost control of your tongue."[7]

Sometimes I have asked folks who say they want to change a bad behavior but insist they can't, "What would you do if someone offered you a million dollars if you successfully avoided raising your voice for a week?" Usually that helps them recognize the fact that their "I can't" beliefs might realistically be replaced with something like, "Yes, I know it would be really hard, and I admit I haven't found a way yet, but it *could* be done if the stakes were high enough."

Remember, only you and I have the power to make positive changes in our PPA. Neither our fiancé nor spouse nor anyone else can make it happen. We also need to keep in mind that none of us can nag or manipulate others into changing, no matter how hard we try. That doesn't mean we should be indifferent when our partner is dealing with a problem, though, as we'll see in the next chapter.

For more help in focusing on personal growth, review chapter 2. See also the personal qualities checklist in appendix C and the agape love inventory in appendix H.

Dan's Two-Part Marriage Improvement Plan

10

Spouse's Problem Area (SPA)

Lecture Less—Listen More

Communication isn't happening unless there is a listener present.

When it comes to addressing issues in our Spouse's Problem Area (SPA), all too often we take the opportunity to *lecture* our partner on what we feel she or he should do, whether our help is asked for or not. Somehow we've come to believe that if we could only get in two more enlightening paragraphs (and if only she or he would pay attention!), we could easily solve all our spouse's problems, whether at work, with their health or weight issues, or in overcoming any or all of their bad habits.

I once heard a wise teacher make the point that *information* is the solution only to the extent that *ignorance* is the problem. Since lack of information is most likely not our spouse's primary problem, the gift of support, care, and love is the response most needed most of the time. So when it comes to the SPA, the goal is not to step in and claim ownership of another's problem but simply to provide support as he or she takes responsibility for any issues they need to resolve. And attentive listening is one of the best ways we can show that kind of support and encouragement.

Good listening isn't just about taking turns talking. Rather, it means giving our full attention to learning from what others are saying, to feel what they feel, to try to see things from their perspective. And like other important skills, this one takes practice, but there's a big payoff in our learning to use this kind of love language.

The three Rs of good listening, in order, are

1. *Reflect*. Take time to let it sink in. Show with body language and facial expressions that we're taking time to respectfully understand, whether or not we agree with what's being said.

2. *Rephrase*. It's often helpful to play back pieces of what we're hearing, as in "You seem to feel pretty mad about how you were treated," or "Sounds like you feel really strongly about that." Such paraphrases serve as perception checks ("Am I hearing you right?") and show that we're actually paying attention.

3. *Respond*. When the other person is completely finished, and there's nothing else they want or need to say at the time, then we might take a turn.

All problems, whether at work or at home, whether frustrations over unfair treatment or distress over hurt feelings, become more manageable when someone simply attends to us in an empathic way. And the simple fact is that communication isn't really happening unless there is some kind of listener present.

Here's what good listening is not:

- It isn't giving advice on what to do.
- It's not telling others how they should feel or not feel.
- It's not trying simply to cheer them up or to distract them.
- It's not telling them that what they're going through is "just like" our own experience.

Some of the above responses may occasionally be appropriate *after* we have listened, but they are not what listening is about.

Lacking the skill of good listening, we are more likely to engage in unproductive communication habits like arguing, in which we take at least partial ownership of someone else's problem and set out to fix it with a lecture. My definition of an argument is when two or more people are trying to talk at the same time—which means there are no real listeners present—and when the main purpose of their speeches is not to inform but to convince or to win. Whenever we are about creating winners and losers, the relationship itself becomes the loser. At least I've seldom seen an argument end with anyone admitting wrong or expressing gratitude for the wonderful enlightenment offered by the other person!

A good thing to remember about arguing is that it always takes two or more to keep one going, and that we can opt out of one at any time. We may disengage by saying something like, "I understand where you're coming from, and I know you're really upset (or worried, or frustrated), but I think I'll just stop now and listen, if that will help." Or if a heated discussion is about a jointly owned problem, to say, "Maybe we should talk about this later when we can take turns hearing each other."

So to exit an argument, calmly stop participating but keep listening. Repeat the above as often as needed. Then move to the Mutual Problem Area (MPA) if necessary, which is the focus of the next chapter.

11

Mutual Problem Area (MPA)

Conflict Is Inevitable—Combat Is Optional

Unless there is a fire or some other emergency, most problems can wait for a mutually agreed-on time and place where we can calmly work them out.

Ever notice how when the phone or doorbell rings, we can miraculously switch from being loud and rude to becoming suddenly quiet and well mannered? It's made me think maybe we should install inside doorbells in our homes that give off similar signals, the kind that would result in our calming down and switching to more mature, respectful communication, the calm, let's-talk-it-over mode needed in the MPA.

But why do married couples experience so much combat in the first place? Why are we usually more courteous toward strangers and neighbors than we are with those we claim to love the most?

When I ask folks these questions, I get responses like these:

- "I'm more likely to let my guard down at home, especially when I'm tired at the end of a day and just need to unwind."
- "I grew up in a yelling and screaming family. Rudeness was the rule rather than the exception, so it's what I do best."
- "I need a safe place to vent when I'm upset. I assume my spouse and family will put up with me and aren't likely to leave me, no matter how badly I behave."
- "My marital and family relationships matter more, and feel more urgent, than almost anything else in my life, hence the intensity or desperation I feel."

To resolve conflicts agreeably, we need to follow this simple rule: Calmly talk things over first, then take time to work out a solution. In this way we focus on two separate parts of the process. Otherwise, responding from habit, we may do the opposite: start with our minds already made up about what we're convinced is right, then spend hours trying to convince the other person to see it our way.

In the MPA, we will not only want to first describe and discuss an issue, but to learn what makes it so important to our partner, what her or his underlying needs and wishes are. That way we slow down the process and show the respect that's so important in any negotiation. And instead of simply reacting to what we've heard, we first make sure we're hearing it right. After this we can brainstorm new ideas that might address the interests and concerns of each partner. In other words, we will always focus on the *problem*, not attack our partner; and act as allies rather than adversaries.

Then we are ready to review the options we've come up with, arrange them in order of preference, and try to come to consensus on a solution we're both willing to try. The following is a summary of good rules to observe in the MPA:

- We will respectfully discuss first, decide later.
- We will take turns being the "speaker" and the "listener." If necessary we will use a "talking stick" (a pen or pencil in hand will do) to indicate who has the floor and can thus talk without interruption.
- Whoever is the speaker will try to be as calm and factual as possible, just giving information about what she or he feels and wants rather than resorting to accusation or manipulation.
- When we are the listener, we will do only that—listen—except for occasionally reflecting back or summarizing what we've heard (perception-checks, as in, "Did I hear you right?").
- We will agree that either of us can ask for a time-out if tensions escalate or if we get into an argument. The person asking for the time out will initiate the time back in within a reasonable time (an hour or so).
- If we fail to come to an agreement, we will adopt an interim solution that remains in place until we come up with a better one, or we will agree to seek help from a third party mediator or counselor if we reach an impasse.

Having regular couple's meetings to work at all of the above can be a good alternative to walking on eggshells and wondering how to introduce sensitive subjects at times when we hope our spouse is in just the right, receptive frame of mind. In mutually planned meetings, we are each committed to staying in that kind of calm and productive mode. Of course, either partner can ask for meetings at other times as needed, with the other spouse either agreeing to have one then and there or offering another time reasonably soon.

The point is to regularly do couple's business in the rational, common sense way we would imagine partners doing in any good jointly managed enterprise. Unless there is a fire or some other kind of emergency, most issues can actually benefit from partners waiting for mutually agreed-on times to work them out.

Here are some "minutes" of a weekly business meeting of a young couple we'll call Fred and Mary, who are following the general outline found in appendix I.

1. *Affirmations:* Fred for finally making a doctor's appointment about his allergy and for preparing a great Sunday dinner. Mary for starting regular exercise and for how she handled a problem at work.
2. *Old business:* Reviewed notes about yard sale plans and a budget for upcoming trip to family reunion. Fred is reminded to follow through on getting prices on a new furnace.
3. *Calendar:* Fred has an overnight business trip Wednesday and Thursday. Mary will lead midweek youth group meeting and make

sure trash gets out the next morning. Fred will get off work early enough Friday to go to an area-wide music festival together. Couple's brunch "date" set for Saturday.
4. *Finances:* Paid end-of-month bills, went over bank statement. How do we get new furnace paid? Will talk about this more next week.
5. *New business:*

a. *Mess and clutter in family room:* Brainstormed a number of ideas, like putting clothes and personal items in a box at the end of each day, to be redeemed with a fine; taking turns with daily cleaning duty, with another small fine for whoever forgets; simply trying harder to keep the room from getting so messy. Couldn't agree on a plan, but will talk over on our Friday evening trip to music festival.
b. *More time to work at our spiritual disciplines together:* After some discussion, agreed to take turns reading some kind of devotional material to the other each evening at bedtime.
c. *Aging car:* Vehicle has 154,000 miles, needs some repairs. Agreed to discuss more next week, but will go ahead with needed repairs.

6. *Next meeting:* Same time next Monday.

For an outline of an agenda to have in hand for the above kind of couple's meeting, see appendix I.

12

When Problems Persist

Seek Help Before Difficulties Become Crises

Ted and Sara (names and details are changed) came for marital help after Sara learned that Ted, a traveling sales rep for his company, was having an emotional affair with a female business colleague. When Sara found the evidence of this through checking Ted's cell phone records and confronted him, he admitted the relationship had gone on for several years, that he had been unhappy in their marriage for a long time, and that he hadn't had the courage to tell her how he felt.

Sara was devastated, not just because of Ted's infidelity, but also because of his lack of honesty with her over so many years. Ted admitted he was wrong for not telling her about what he was needing in the marriage and also acknowledged that none of their marital problems justified what he had done or his having covered it up.

After long hours of intense talks and months of individual

and marriage therapy, they finally reached a turning point in their relationship. Ted, desperate to save their marriage, agreed to meet regularly with a mentor, a trusted older friend of theirs, for ongoing accountability and support. The couple agreed to regular couple's meetings together and quarterly checkups with their marriage counselor.

Meanwhile, they realized some of the costs they could have spared themselves if they had sought help earlier: (1) a year of intense conflict and distress in their marriage, (2) a profound loss of trust that took a long time to regain, (3) feelings of humiliation as close friends and family members became aware of what happened, (4) attorney fees as each prepared for the worst, (5) extensive professional counseling for them as individuals and as a couple.

In the end, they felt blessed and relieved that they were able to salvage their marriage. At their last session, they shared the story of how a pair of white doves had recently chosen their upstairs bedroom window ledge as a nightly roosting place. It was a heaven-sent sign, they felt, of the return of a healing peace that they hadn't experienced in years.

By the time many distressed couples agree to go for counseling, they feel so bruised and resentful they wonder if they will ever be able to mend all that's gone wrong. Issues that could have been addressed as simple maintenance problems escalate to the level where they require a major overhaul. Worse yet, one or both partners may decide the hassle isn't worth it and may decide to trade in their marriage for something (or *someone*) they hope will work out better.

But before even thinking of burning any marital bridges, it's important to realize that the grass on the other side of the proverbial fence is seldom as green as it appears. In a 1998 South Carolina Marital Health study, 62 percent of divorced adults polled wished they had tried harder to keep their marriage together. The same study found that 76 percent of those divorced believed that in choosing divorce, people typically trade one set of problems for another, compared to 67 percent of the general population supporting that belief.[8]

Unless there is a serious and chronic case of adultery, abuse, or addiction for which one or both spouses are refusing help, it's almost always preferable to salvage an existing relationship rather than to simply leave it behind, unresolved. And we now know that divorce rates for second marriages are even higher than for first ones. Besides, many a separated couple's original problems continue or get worse through custody battles, support and visitation disputes, and around holidays, birthdays, graduations, and weddings of children and grandchildren until death do them part.

So from both a biblical and a practical point of view, paying attention to resolving problems before they get out of hand and result in a breakup is a wise thing.

Here are some early warning signs that a relationship might need outside help:

- Your close friends or other family members express concerns about your relationship.

- Your children or other significant people in your life are being affected by your problems.
- You are experiencing a lot of emotional distress in the form of depression or feelings of despair.
- The joy has gone out of your lovemaking, or your love life is nonexistent.
- One or the other begins to bring up separation or divorce, even if just in the heat of a conflict.
- You continue to have the same bruising conflicts over and over, and are getting nowhere in resolving them.
- Your fights become physically and/or verbally abusive (involving hitting, yelling, name calling).

Life is far too short not to get pastoral or professional help when serious problems begin to dominate a relationship.

For a list of things to look for in a marriage counselor, see appendix J.

Part III

Maintenance Through the Minivan Years

The God of your father—may he help you!
And may The Strong God—may he give you his blessings,
Blessings tumbling out of the skies,
blessings bursting up from the Earth—
blessings of breasts and womb.
May the blessings of your father
exceed the blessings of the ancient mountains,
surpass the delights of the eternal hills.

—Genesis 49:25-26 (The Message)

13

Park at a Congregation Near You

Join Others in Pursuit of a Healthy Marriage and Family

While distressed marriages often benefit from professional help, every marriage needs the kind of help and support offered by members of a good congregational family.

Which causes more stress—going from being single to married, or from being married to having children?

Most parents will agree it is the latter. Much as Alma Jean and I looked forward to having a family, nothing fully prepared us for the demands of bearing and rearing children, or for the challenge it created for our marriage. Not that we would want to change anything about having our three, and not that becoming a family made our marriage worse. It simply made it different and more difficult—but ultimately a lot richer and better. We realize that much of what made child rearing so stressful was that this was the one area of our lives where we absolutely did not want to fail.

For most of our parenting years, I was a busy pastor and part-time teacher, and we lived in a parsonage across from our church. Between the demands of church work and living in our congregation's glass house, we had more than our share of tensions. Even if I hadn't been a pastor, I would have still needed to work at balancing the energy needed for our church family and for our own, given my tendency to become overcommitted and overinvolved in things.

Increasingly I hear people resolving this tension with, "We've decided our family comes first," referring, of course, to their nuclear family. In practice this often means parents taking on fewer church responsibilities, taking more family vacations on weekends, and rarely joining in congregational activities other than on Sunday mornings when they are in town.

I support the need to set reasonable priorities, but I am concerned whenever church participation gets put further and further down the list of after-school activities, soccer practice, music lessons, and a multitude of other events and meetings. Or when increased time vegetating around the family's entertainment center takes precedence over maintaining good connections with friends and fellow church members. Part of the problem, Tom Sine says, is that "the identity of the church and the meaning of community for many have become hopelessly confused with buildings, budgets, programs, personalities, and—regrettably—even the self-seeking values of American culture."[9]

Assuming a concept of church as a community of like-minded folks committed to caring for each other, it is shortsighted to pit biological family against church family. Why? Because having a people who are our spiritual sisters and brothers, and who become spiritual cousins and uncles and aunts and grandparents for our children, is more important than ever in our minivan years. Our marriages are less likely to thrive, or even survive, if our families aren't being well nurtured.

While ailing marriages and families can often benefit from professional help, all of them need the kind of regular first-aid offered by members of their biological and spiritual families. In fact, I see a direct correlation between the growing number of marriage breakups and the increased breakdown of this kind of community and extended family support. When couples lack access to wise elders and peers with whom they can share their distresses and from whom they can gain much-needed encouragement and help, even small problems can become overwhelming.

During the minivan years, many of these problems have to do with child rearing itself. Wise couples realize their need for the blessing and support of a whole congregation in order to raise a whole and healthy family. My own parents felt so strongly about this that they made a fourteen-hundred-mile move with eight children to become a part of a faith community they believed would have a better influence on us.

Their sacrifice paid off. While the church community they chose may not have offered much in the way of polished worship services, great preaching, or eye-catching Sunday-school material, it provided something far more important. The congregation offered lots of support in the form of frequent, warm hospitality and time spent working together at harvests and building or quilting projects, all of which were associated with good meals, conversations, and story telling. It was in those settings and from these church-family mentors that I gained many of my values. I still love these good people and cherish their memories.

In rearing our own three children, we are forever indebted to the good church people who invited our family into their hearts and homes, and many others who loved us, took an interest in our children, and made a positive impact on us all. We could not have done it without them.

Yet I see very few books and articles on marriage or family life even mentioning a larger context than that of the nuclear family unit of mother, father, and 2.3 children, with an occasional visit by doting grandparents. The underlying notion is that parents do this by themselves, and they alone get the credit (or the blame) for how their children turn out.

So how can we work together to help our children grow in their faith and in their commitment to God and the church? Here are some important ways:

- Both at home and with our church family, we celebrate lots of love, joy, peace, and other good Spirit fruit. We realize that as a community we need to demonstrate the same kind of "gleam in the eye" enthusiasm for serving God and the church we want our children to have.
- We cultivate good relationships with others in our congregations by taking time for warm, stress-free connections and conversations with each other and with each other's children.

- As much as possible, we make childcare arrangements with other members of our church family or with other folks who share and reinforce our values.
- We try hard to be in agreement with our spouse (and with other parents in our church as much as possible) in setting reasonable expectations and guidelines for involvement in church and youth group activities—without either compromising our positions or engaging in ongoing power struggles.
- We plan for vacation and other family activities that involve the larger church family, such as service projects, camping experiences, and attendance at churchwide assemblies that expose our children to as many good people of faith as possible.
- Meanwhile, we reduce, rather than increase, access to the many forms of entertainment available that compete for good family and church time.

In short, we remember we simply can't do all of this on our own. We realize it does take a whole congregation to sustain a good marriage and to raise a whole and healthy family.

At mid-life, John and Jane revise their parent wish list

14

Avoid Power and Courage Failures

Maintain Personal Stature, Empowerment, and Protection

The more empowered and secure we feel, the more calmly and effectively we can behave.

In family counseling sessions, I've sometimes had each participant draw a stick figure portrait of members of their household, indicating by height how much power or influence they see each person having. Where relationships are going well, spouses tend to picture themselves and their mates as having equal standing and their children as having levels of stature and influence appropriate to their age. They recognize, of course, that being equal doesn't mean being identical, in that each individual has unique roles, strengths, and abilities, but members of healthy families see themselves as helping to raise each other to positions of ever-higher value and empowerment.

In conflict-filled households, people are more likely to see themselves as diminished and intimidated by others, most of whom they see as having more stature and standing than themselves. It often comes as a surprise to discover how different, even opposite, people's perceptions of each other can be in the same family. A husband, for example, may in a marriage counseling session express the belief that his wife has considerably more psychological and other forms of power and control than he, while she sees things in exactly the opposite way.

Whether accurate or not, each person's perceptions become their reality. And since most conflicts are more about trying to equalize a perceived imbalance of power than about addressing the actual issues in question, it's easy to see how these skewed perceptions tend to feed ongoing power struggles. This is why feeling adequately empowered is so important in maintaining healthy and happy ties.

Feeling *under*-empowered is the normal experience of most of us during our growing-up years. Throughout my own childhood, I often daydreamed about what it would be like to become a full-fledged adult, to finally be in charge of my own very successful life. As a teen, I even borrowed a Charles Atlas body-building course, complete with assurances that a slender and not so athletic kid like myself could become a muscular macho man. But after months of effort, I still felt and looked small. I was focusing on the *outside* instead of the *inside* part of growing up.

I was in my early forties when I finally asked myself, with some help from a spiritual director I had at the time, how much longer I was going to feel like an inexperienced novice instead of the confident, capable adult I had the right and responsibility to be. It dawned on me that when my father was in *his* forties, I saw him as having the stature of a Moses coming off Mount Sinai. Of course he probably didn't feel the part, but he had me convinced that a forty-year-old is someone to be respected and reckoned with.

Later in life I learned I wasn't alone in feeling I had less stature and status than others in my circle of adult peers. Part of me felt that was how it should be. Wasn't I supposed to put myself in a lower, humbler position than others, including my spouse? Perhaps, but healthy humility means to choose that place from a position of strength, not inferiority, to respect oneself and every other child of God as equally and incomparably precious, neither above us or below us. This means avoiding even a "humbler than thou" attitude, since in God's eyes, we are all on the same level pedestal.

Maintaining this kind of capable peer feeling is vital to a good marriage through the minivan years. As parents, for example, we need to be sure to claim a full sense of adult power and stature, not in order to lord it over our children, but to *lead* them. Our mandate is to *bring up* our sons and daughters, to *raise* and empower them to become strong leaders and eventually good parents themselves, not simply to "keep them in their place."

The good news is that the more empowered each of us feels, the more calmly and effectively we can behave. We no longer have to resort to manipulation or depend on our adrenaline-driven anger to give us the feeling of having the adequate, adult stature and standing that is already ours.

In Paul's letter to the Ephesians, we are repeatedly promised power to spare, again not power *over* others but a supernatural ("more than we can ask or imagine," 3:20) "might" that we can experience *with* others. In addition, we are told we are in "every way" (1:23) to grow up to experience the "full stature of Christ" himself (4:13 NRSV).

It gets even better. A final promise given in the Ephesians letter is that of adequate protection (armor) against spiritual or emotional harm (see 6: 10-17). In our relationships, I think of that as a lot like being prepared for bad weather. We can't control unpleasant climate or road conditions, but we can be equipped with a well-maintained vehicle, a working heater, and the kind of attire that gives us whatever protection we need. In a similar way, to better cope with others' disturbing behaviors, we need to make sure we're ready for any storminess they may create. Good protection allows us to actually be closer to family members and others who are contributing to a bad day without risking our own safety or losing our own serenity. We can thus learn to both like them better and to feel less vulnerable and intimidated around them.

I once heard someone say, "There's no such thing as bad weather, only inadequate protection." With that mindset we can stop seeing our spouse, children, or others as being our problem, but instead see the problem as one of being able to maintain the full stature, plentiful power, and adequate protection necessary for carrying our own good weather with us.

An intimidated Jill's perception of power balance in the marriage.

Husband Ron's perception.

15

Chart Memorable Paths

Pass on Faith and Values with Traditions and Rituals

The supper smoke is coming blue out of the chimney, and the window in the kitchen shows yellow. The house looks so incredibly cozy and desirable in the midst of this fiercely beautiful and merciless landscape; it is enough to tear your soul out by its roots. Into my mind comes the realization that here I am, now, out of all time and space, here in this place. And I say to myself, This is my home. My woman. A baby. Two babies. Simple things like that.[10]

—Elliott Merrick

At every phase of life, we are creating memories. All of the positive experiences we have together as couples in some way enrich our children's lives and prepare them for better relationships of their own. And whatever memorable times we enjoy with our offspring can greatly enrich our marriage. In God's economy, every blessing and every trial we experience can add to and even multiply our assets, rather than resulting in subtraction and division.

Studies show a positive correlation between couples establishing good routines and rituals and their enjoying more marital and family satisfaction.[11] Children in that kind of environment experience better health, stronger family ties, and a more positive sense of personal worth and identity.

In *Parenting for the '90s*, Philip Osborne stressed the importance of spending lots of problem-free time with children, enjoying bedtime rituals, family trips, and frequent get-togethers with good friends and relatives. It is through these kinds of experiences, he believes, that we do our most effective work in passing on good values and creating good memories.

In his book *Great Possessions: An Amish Farmer's Journal*, David Kline describes some of the simple everyday pleasures of living on his family's 120-acre Holmes County, Ohio, farm. Without the distractions of radio, television, e-mail, or cell phones, something as ordinary as going for walks together or having the whole family involved in shocking their newly cut wheat on a cool June evening becomes an opportunity for family fun and conversation.[12]

Few of us may ever experience the benefits of that kind of simple, rural lifestyle, but we *can* radically reduce time spent with passive forms of entertainment and engage in more active work, play, and conversations together. For example, we can make sure we enjoy at least one leisurely meal with each other every day. Columnist Luann Austin writes, "Gathering around a table to share a meal is a daily sacrament we often take for granted. . . . As we partake of the meal, we partake of each other."[13]

All of this takes time. Though someone has written a book called *365 Ways to Save Time with Kids*, what we are more likely to need in our fast-paced culture is to find more ways of *savoring* time rather than just *saving* it. In fact, we would do well to squander it sometimes with our spouse, with a child, or with a friend, simply enjoying each other's closeness, marveling over a sunset or an ant colony, or sharing a story or personal experience.

Alma Jean and I have especially fond memories of regular story times with our children at bedtime when they were young. Other rituals included a tradition of having a resident of a nearby home for the handicapped at our house for Christmas Eve and for an annual birthday dinner, and of enjoying a mouthwatering family brunch every Christmas morning, always prepared by our second-oldest son. Other simple rituals include waving goodbye from our living room window whenever any of us drives off, even for an errand, and the long-standing habit Alma Jean and I have of reading and praying together before we drift off to sleep.

Throughout the minivan years, we need all the time and help possible to maintain healthy relational bonds. Here are some additional examples of good family and marital traditions:

- Garden together, and preserve, prepare, and serve home-cooked meals.
- Make bedtimes occasions for story telling, reading, and/or prayers together.
- Develop traditions around holidays, birthdays, and anniversaries of special family events.
- Share family hobbies, interests, and recreational activities.
- Do service projects together.
- Take part in congregational activities.
- Sponsor a needy child abroad.
- Attend churchwide assemblies and other events.
- Host international students and guests from other lands and cultures.
- Regularly attend family reunions, and find other ways of staying in touch with extended family members.

Life is too short not to experience the closest and most memorable connections possible with those we care about most.

16

Observe Time-Honored Rules of the Road

Protect Against Threats of Infidelity

Genesis-old, congregationally supported fences around sex and marriage are certainly as important as laws governing driving.

We all agree children need rules: Wait your turn. Always tell the truth. Keep your promises. Eat your vegetables before dessert. But do we grownups need some similar dos and don't's in maintaining faithful marriage and family relationships?

Some would have us believe that congregations and individuals don't need to focus on boundaries so much if they practice living from their center, their own core values. Cultivate a healthy relationship with God and with your marriage partner, they say, and you won't find yourself straying, just as providing cattle with good water and pasture means not having to worry so much about maintaining strong fences.

There's certainly some truth to that, but on the farm where I grew up, our herds needed both good food *and* good fences. Even with lots of green grass on their side of the fence, our animals would sometimes break into adjoining fields to feast on some even greener-looking corn or clover. The results were ruinous both to the health of the cattle and the condition of our crops.

Without good boundaries, all too many married persons, including trusted pastors and other professionals, have experienced (and inflicted) untold devastation and harm. And in a whole society that disregards good boundary markers at will, folks are hooking up and breaking up in ever-greater numbers, resulting not only in severe heartbreaks but also in career disasters, financial headaches, fractured families, and emotionally bruised children.

Experience tells us that an ounce of prevention is better than a pound of cure—or a ton of regret. So the Calvary Community Church, a large African-American congregation in Hampton, Virginia, has come up with "Ten Commitments to Righteousness" for its young people. These include unapologetic statements like "You shall not be sexually active until marriage." Certainly we parents and other married folks need equally strong boundary markers.

To me, Genesis-old, congregationally supported fences around sex and marriage are at least as necessary as rules governing driving. Should we consider it a violation of our freedom if we're bound by dozens of common-sense traffic laws every day?

On my way to work, for example, I don't arbitrarily choose which side of the road I drive on, and I always observe the stop sign at the end of Hamlet Drive before I enter the highway. As I head toward town, I endeavor to slow my speed to forty-five miles per hour, then thirty-five, for everyone's safety and protection, and I wait as needed at several traffic lights before crossing the intersection. All the while I display a license plate on my vehicle and carry a driver's license in my wallet. Just a piece of paper, some may say, but one that serves a legitimate and useful purpose.

Somehow I fail to find these rules restrictive. Good boundaries are not roadblocks but safeguards that give me the freedom to get from point A to point B with far less hassle—and a lot less risk of having a wreck.

Since I know that a bad one of those could *really* rob me of my freedom, I suggest the following defensive driving rules for a safer marital journey:

- Any affection shown toward co-workers, friends, or members of our church family is subject to similar rules that apply to members of our biological families (for example, no prolonged hugging or secretive displays of affection).
- We avoid any personal Internet or phone communication except with folks we and our spouse both know and trust, and about whom we are willing to share the full content of our conversations.

- We do not tolerate the use of pornography of any kind and rule out entertaining any sexual fantasies other than those involving our spouse.
- We carefully monitor the kinds of entertainment we allow in our home and in our personal life. If we don't want our kids to watch something, we probably shouldn't watch it ourselves.
- We make ourselves morally accountable not only to our spouse but also to at least one other adult whom we ask to regularly check on us as to how we are maintaining good boundaries.

All of the above may seem like a lot of work, but it is absolutely worth it if we can avoid the untold harm unfaithfulness inflicts on our marriage and our children.

17

End Road Rage and Reckless Driving

Keep Relationship Accounts Short

Of course there was the anger where the love is strong.
It spilled like gasoline.
It's crude, but it's a power we can draw upon
if it fuels the right machine.[14]

—David Wilcox

A woman in Panama City, Florida, got so mad at her husband for ignoring her that she grabbed a cigarette lighter and set one of his shirts on fire. Problem was, the blaze got out of control and burned down their house. This did get her husband's attention, but it also resulted in the couple losing most of their worldly possessions. To make matters worse, their insurance company refused to cover the loss, since the blaze was set intentionally by one of the owners. And as if this weren't bad enough, the wife, described by the investigator as "a nice lady with a temper," was charged with second-degree arson. As is often the case, the couple's original argument was over a minor issue, the passive-aggressive husband's main crime being that of merely lying in bed and totally tuning out his wife's complaints. This got her so upset she decided to apply the lighter.

The moral of the story is clear: whatever immediate satisfaction we may get from impulsively venting our rage can be spoiled by unforeseen negative consequences.

Unfortunately, a lot of popular psychology has promoted the idea that repressing any emotions, especially angry ones, is A Very Bad Thing. We are admonished to let it all out, to let other people "have it," if necessary, in order to relieve ourselves of some terrible poison that can allegedly cause high blood pressure, depression, anxiety, and all kinds of other problems.

But does "letting it all out" really help our marriage, family, or other relationships?

The notion that keeping any anger inside is bad for you is based loosely on Sigmund Freud's theory that our subconscious mind is a reservoir for repressed sexual instincts. Many therapists in the 1960s and 1970s simply took that a step further and urged us to avoid repressing all kinds of feelings, especially angry ones.

More recent researchers, such as psychologist Carol Travis, author of

Anger, the Misunderstood Emotion, disagree. Travis insists that even Freud never argued that the suppression of instincts was always bad but was actually necessary for society's survival. "Without it," she asks, "who would mind the store, build the bridges, create the Mona Lisa?" Nor does she recommend things like punching pillows, throwing plates, or screaming at people as ways of "getting anger out." She believes that such actions result in little more than "Sure, it didn't solve anything, but it made me feel better."[15]

My question is whether just feeling better should be our primary goal as grownups. What if it makes our spouse or other loved ones feel worse? What if it damages our relationship with our children while at the same time fails to address the real problems that are bothering us?

We are told in Scripture, "'In your anger do not sin': Do not let the sun go down while you are still angry" (Ephesians 4:26). In other words, don't go to bed angry. Angry feelings can be okay but are never an excuse for harbored resentments, hurtful behaviors or just plain bad judgment.

In an emergency like a fire or an accident, the release of large doses of adrenaline can be useful. In most other situations, however, our God-given anger energy is better harnessed as emotional fuel to drive a well-tuned, carefully controlled engine, one that transforms anger-power into a useful purpose, giving us the courage and the motivation to find workable solutions to our problems.

Rabbi Joseph Telushkin writes, "That you feel rage does not entitle you to inflict emotional pain on others any more than feelings of sexual attraction entitle you to rape the source of your attraction."[16]

Here are some biblical and time-proven ways of managing anger productively:

- *Relax:* Unless there is an immediate crisis, give yourself a time-out to cool off. Count to ten. Let the anger subside. "Those with good sense are slow to anger, and it is their glory to overlook an offense" (Proverbs 19:11 NRSV).
- *Release:* Breathe deeply. Let go of excess hostility. Engage in healthy exercise. "Put away from you all bitterness and wrath and anger" (Ephesians 4:31 NRSV).
- *Reframe:* Instead of taking everyone's behaviors personally, try to think of what might be some of the needs behind their actions. Then work at ways of attacking problems rather than people. "[Love] is not irritable or resentful" (1 Corinthians 13:5 NRSV).
- *Rephrase:* Turn negative reactions into helpful, problem-solving responses. Offer useful information instead of hurtful accusation. Engage in negotiation rather than heated argument. "Let no evil talk come out of your mouths, but only what is useful for building up" (Ephesians 4:29 NRSV).
- *Forgive:* Recognize repentance in others and be ready to relieve them of debts they owe you, just as you would have them forgive you your offenses. Even if there is no repentance, it is better to let go of uncollectible debts rather than harbor ill will and resentment. "Be kind to one another, tenderhearted, forgiving one another, as God in Christ has forgiven you" (Ephesians 4:32 NRSV).

I'M WITH GUILTY
He Did It.
9/26
SESSION NOTES:
schedule more sessions

18

Be Friends Forever

Maintain Your Marriage for Life

My beloved "bird in the hand" is worth far more to me
than any other I could have chosen,
a priceless gift that keeps on giving.

Our second-oldest, Brent, wrote the following after he and his wife of less than two years went for a walk one night that took them through a snow-covered cemetery:

> There is such a remarkable transformation of our little world when blanketed by several inches of frozen moisture. The reflection of light from the white crust creates a surreal illumination of otherwise unnoticed objects under the night sky. . . . There is a silence that is in part due to the lack of people

> venturing out but primarily caused by the muffling of sound, as if the world was covered by a heavy blanket. Within this silence, surrounded by the ghosts of lives that no longer wake up, see the sun, or smell the crispness of new snow, I find myself reflecting on the seemingly brief moment that constitutes our time on this earth.
>
> Now I am home, typing away in my small but cozy apartment in a little house in a little town, in a little moment that relative to the scheme of time is small and insignificant. But within this moment I have a clarity that compels me to hold my wife's hand a little tighter, scratch my dogs' bellies a little longer, thank God for the blessings in my life and not complain about the problems, and tell my friends that I love them very much and thank them for being a part of indelible memories that bring warmth and light to my life as the night's snow continues to fall.

I was moved as I read this. It reminded me that it is often these ordinary experiences that make us realize how blessed we are with gifts like marriage, family, and friendships.

I remember once hearing of a successfully married couple who, when asked, "When did your friendship end and your love begin?" replied, "Ah, but that is our secret. Our friendship never ended."

Friendship is so important because, when all is said and done, it is not primarily the romantic aspect of our relationship that gives it life as much as an enduring sense of companionship and closeness. Romance, like the sweets and fats at the peak of the Food Pyramid I grew up with, can make for very tasty dishes and desserts, but a Relationship Pyramid needs much more than that. At its base we need lots of the daily bread of God's great unconditional love. In the middle of the pyramid we need nourishing entrees in the form of regular experiences of partnership, companionship, and friendship—the greatest of these being friendship.

Relationship Pyramid

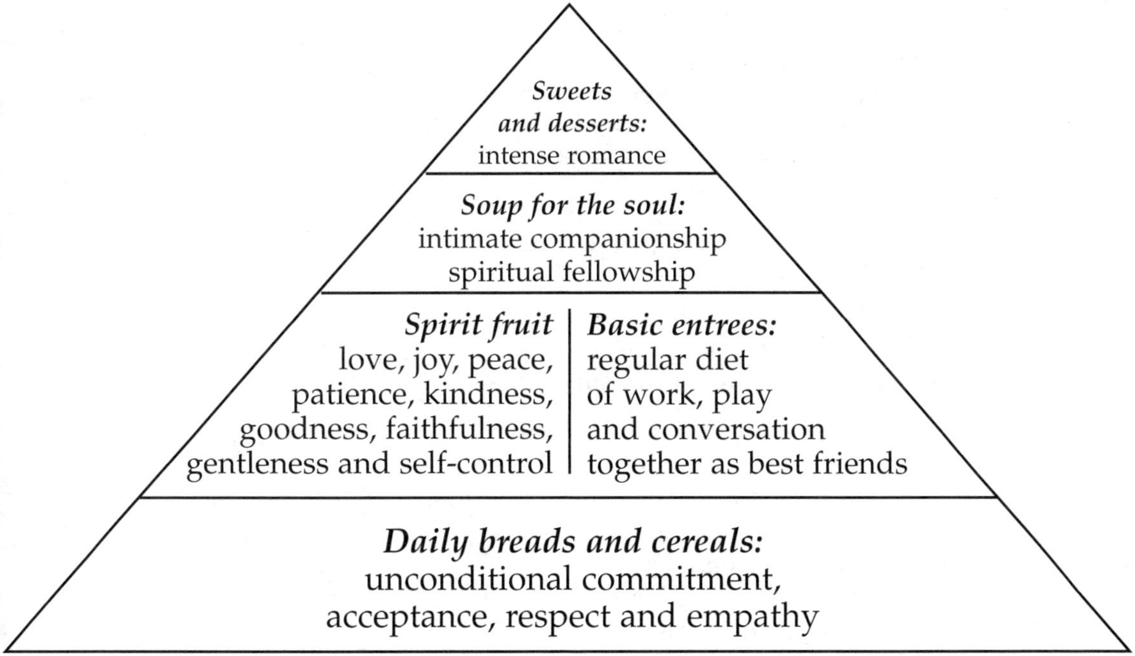

Sweets and desserts:
intense romance

Soup for the soul:
intimate companionship
spiritual fellowship

Spirit fruit	***Basic entrees:***
love, joy, peace, patience, kindness, goodness, faithfulness, gentleness and self-control	regular diet of work, play and conversation together as best friends

Daily breads and cereals:
unconditional commitment,
acceptance, respect and empathy

Years ago my wife made me a homemade Valentine-shaped card on which she pasted the following clipping from an old magazine, a piece called "Settling In," by an unidentified author.

> I have settled into love
> The way that houses settle
>   Plaster slightly cracked
>   Floors a little tilted
> But still this love is home.
>
> It's really rather sweet
> A kind of fire-in-the-fireplace love
>   Charred a little
>   Singed from time to time
> But still this love burns strong.
>
> I do not know. Maybe this is all
> That I will ever have
> A sort of old house, slow fire love,
> But it gives me such pleasure
> That I do not long for Roman candles.
>
> For in the joining, in the sweetness,
> In the holding of our love
> There is no sense of strangeness.
> There is no dislocation,
> For no matter where we are
> If we're together, it is home.
> And look, my dear, just over there—
> I think I see a Roman candle!

This card, one of my prized possessions, expresses some of the joy I feel in being a part of Alma Jean's life. She is my beloved "bird in the hand," worth so much more to me than any other I could have chosen. In our present state, I can't imagine anyone who could so bless me, stand by me, love me—and yes, sometimes irritate and annoy me, just as I do her. But she is a priceless asset, a gift that just keeps on giving.

I close with some reflections I wrote after our fortieth wedding anniversary, which also is a summary of much of what I have tried to say in this owners' manual.

If I Had Forty More Years of Marriage
Thanks to a gracious God and a long-suffering wife, I've learned a lot during our four decades together. So if I could have forty more years . . .
. . . I would choose the same incomparably good woman and put more effort into cherishing her as my most special, capable, and precious friend.
. . . I would drop all conditions for *loving*. I would more fully accept and love her as God does each of us, flaws and all.
. . . I would maintain reasonable conditions for *living*. I would expect us to negotiate our disagreements, respect our boundaries, and honor our promises.
. . . I would invest more time and energy in expanding (and celebrating) the problem-free parts of our life together. As much as possible, I would guard those times from intrusion and interruption.
. . . I would take more responsibility for my contributions to problems in our marriage. Working on these would keep me

busy and would help most to bring about the good changes I want to see in our relationship.

. . . I would become less focused on my partner's shortcomings. I would try to show support and empathy but also work at helping "fix" things for her only if and when invited.

. . . I would practice doing more listening (and less lecturing) when my partner is talking. As a listener, I would focus on trying to understand where she is coming from (even if I disagreed) and not immediately try to steer the conversation in another direction. Instead of interrupting, I would do my best to stay in the listening mode until she is finished.

. . . When it is my turn to talk, I would use less accusation, blame, and criticism, and simply offer information about how I'm seeing something, how I'm feeling, and what I'm needing. I would use more periods after my sentences—and fewer question marks and exclamation points—and not go on and on after I've made a point (except when giving affirmations and appreciations!).

. . . I would regularly, or whenever needed, make myself available for civil, one-on-one couple's meetings to iron out problems between us, then try to address these as calmly and effectively as possible (in order to get back to more of our fun, no-problem times). I would seek outside help if needed to be able to better do this.

. . . I would focus more on using "soft power" in the form of polite requests and attempts to influence, and less of the "hard power" of argument, pressure, and attempts to control.

. . . I would spend more time working, playing, and praying with her, even if it meant less time at the office or for other pursuits.

. . . I would work daily at keeping my . . .
respect *high* (to treat her as I want to be treated),
my expectations *medium* (to celebrate progress but accept imperfections),
and my anxiety *low* (to behave as calmly and maturely as possible).

Finally, to each of my readers, whether single, married for years, recently wed, or thinking of marriage in the future, I pass on this portion of my favorite Irish blessing:

May the blessing of earth—the good, rich earth—be with you.
May you ever have a kindly greeting for those you pass
as you go along its roads.
May the earth be soft under you when you rest upon it,
tired at the end of the day.
May the earth rest easy over you when at the last you lie under it.
May the earth rest so lightly over you
that your spirit may be out from under it quickly,
and up, and off, and on its way to God.[17]

Another helpful book on marriage maintenance is Monday Marriage: Celebrating the Ordinary *by Gerald W. and L. Marlene Kaufman available at www.heraldpress.com/books/mondaymarriage.htm.*

Appendixes

Some Spare Parts

Any materials in these appendixes may be copied for personal use and can also be downloaded at www.flrc.org/lastingmarriage.htm.

A. Bible Texts on Marriage

B. A Family of Origin Inventory

C. A Nine-Point Inventory of Good Personal and Marital Qualities

D. Some 'To Knot or Not to Knot?' Questions

E. Some Wedding Planning Ideas

F. Jesus' Teachings About Money in the Sermon on the Mount

G. Identifying Four Problem and Responsibility Areas

H. Agape Love Inventory

I. Agenda for Regular Couple's Meetings

J. Things to Look for in a Marriage Counselor

K. A Prenuptial Covenant

L. Summary of Homework Ideas for the Four Problem Areas

Appendix A
Bible Texts on Marriage

Genesis 2:18. *The LORD God said, "It is not good for the man to be alone. I will make a helper suitable for him."* The Hebrew word for "helper" does not denote an inferior, but is the same as in psalm texts that state "The Lord is my helper."

Genesis 2:24. *For this reason a man will leave his father and mother and be united to his wife, and they will become one flesh.* This text is quoted by both Jesus and Paul, with Jesus adding, *Therefore what God has joined together, let no one separate* (Matthew 19:6 NRSV).

Exodus 20:14. *You shall not commit adultery.* This is clearly more than a mere suggestion.

Proverbs 18:22. *He who finds a wife finds what is good and receives favor from the LORD.*

Matthew 5:32. *Anyone who divorces his wife, except for marital unfaithfulness, causes her to become an adulteress, and anyone who marries the divorced woman commits adultery.* Jesus considers marriage a serious commitment indeed. See also 19:9.

Ephesians 5:21-22, 25. *Submit to one another out of reverence for Christ. Wives submit to your husbands as to the Lord. . . . Husbands, love your wives, just as Christ loved the church and gave himself up for her.* Each is asked to freely and sacrificially yield to the other.

Colossians 3:18-19. *Wives, submit to your husbands, as is fitting in the Lord. Husbands, love your wives and do not be harsh with them.*

Hebrews 13:4. *Marriage should be honored by all, and the marriage bed kept pure, for God will judge the adulterer and all the sexually immoral.* Unfaithfulness is never an option.

Peter 2:13-14, 17; 3:1, 7. *Submit yourselves for the Lord's sake to every authority . . . whether to the king . . . or to governors. . . . Show proper respect to everyone: Love the brotherhood of believers, fear God, honor the king. . . . Wives, in the same way, be submissive to your husbands so that, if any of them do not believe in the word, they may be won over without words by the behavior of their wives. . . . Husbands, in the same way be considerate as you live with your wives, and treat them with respect as the weaker partner and as heirs with you of the gracious gift of life, so that nothing will hinder your prayers.* The words translated *honor* and *respect* here are from the same Greek root, in this context suggesting that partners honor and respect each other as they would royalty.

Appendix B
A Family of Origin Inventory

Leave any item *blank* if it was not at all true in your family. Use a 1 for every item that was somewhat or occasionally true, a 2 if it was frequently or mostly true, or a 3 if it was very much so or almost always true. Compare and discuss your answers with your fiancé or spouse.

1. Our Family's Love Language

___touch ___praise ___teasing ___surprises
___hugs ___special events ___special favors

2. Ways of Handling Conflicts

___avoid or deny, be nice at any price ___yell and argue
___calmly discuss and negotiate

3. Memories

___don't talk about the past ___share freely and positively
___talk only about past grievances

4. Emotions

___keep them to yourself ___express explosively and dramatically
___report feelings in an honest, up-to-date way

5. Attitudes About Money

___a constant point of tension ___ a relaxed attitude of contentment
___wealth is for sharing ___wealth is for hoarding

6. Work

___perfection is a minimum requirement
___personal worth based on how much you get done
___work seen as a curse ___work celebrated as worthwhile and good

7. Social Activities

___value your privacy, stay at home or with your family
___have lots of friends, entertain often, go out a lot

8. Order and Organization

___"a place (and time) for everything, everything in its place"
___"cleanliness is next to godliness"
___some clutter acceptable, but order appreciated
___chaos and clutter everywhere

9. Attitudes Toward Sex
___didn't talk about it ___inappropriate sex talk and behavior
___positive attitudes and values

10. Gender Roles
___male dominated ___female dominated
___rigid gender roles ___flexible roles

11. Child Rearing
___very strict, firm ___harsh, lots of physical punishment
___verbal or physical abuse ___fair, reasonable discipline
___permissive, anything goes

12. Church, Religion
___strong faith, backed by consistent practice
___strong profession, inconsistent life
___little or no emphasis on religion or church

13. Illnesses or Injuries
___grin and bear it, don't make a big deal of it
___appropriate empathy, support
___use for exerting control, generating sympathy, or establishing martyr or victim status

14. Family Sins, Wrongdoings, Mistakes
___inflict shame, assign blame ___deny, cover up, minimize, keep secret
___confess, forgive, let go

Traits associated with impulses and craving in the lower brain:

sexual immorality, impurity, debauchery, hatred, discord, jealousy, fits of rage, selfish ambition, dissensions, fractions and envy, orgies, drunkenness, and the like

Traits associated with a Spirit-controlled higher brain:

love, peace, joy, patience, kindness, goodness, faithfulness, gentleness, and self-control

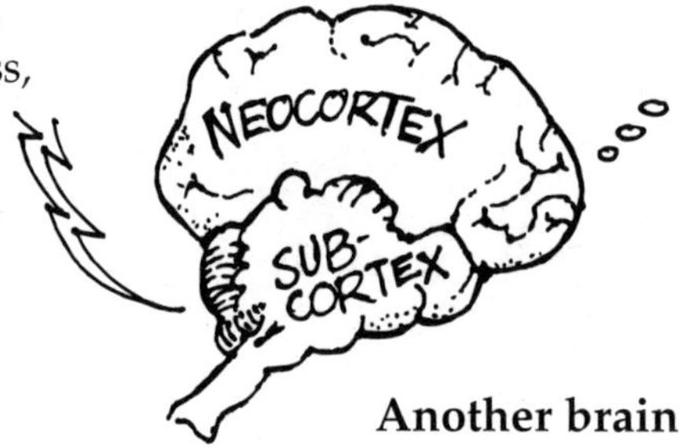

Another brain scan (based on Galatians 5:19-23)

Appendix C
A Nine-Point Inventory of Good Personal and Marital Qualities

Rate yourself on a scale of 0 to 5 as to how much you experience each of the following fruit of the Spirit (from Galatians 5:22-23), which are vital to a good, healthy relationship. You may also want to give your fiancé, mate, or trusted friend the same list to fill out as they see you. Then work at a personal plan for growing more of each of these qualities.

___Love—I am able to be gracious and caring toward others in spite of their actions.

___Joy—I demonstrate a contagiously positive spirit, even in trying circumstances.

___Peace—I experience a deep sense of inner well-being in spite of stresses in my life.

___Patience—I have the calm and strength to endure things (hold on, not give up) even under stress.

___Kindness—I consistently show respect and care toward others, no matter how I'm treated.

___Goodness—I am able to act positively toward others, for their good, even when I am tired or am tempted to hurt them or get even.

___Faithfulness—I have an unwavering commitment to others' good and to the strengthening of my relationships.

___Gentleness—I operate from a reservoir of inner strength that keeps me from resorting to aggressive or desperate actions, even when tested.

___Self-control—I am able to live a calm, controlled, and reasonably well-managed life most of the time.

Appendix D
Some 'To Knot or Not to Knot?' Questions and Inventories

1. For panel members:

- What do you wish you would have known more about yourself or your partner before you married?
- What were some of the more difficult adjustments you had to make as a couple?
- What were some of the greatest surprises you experienced after you were married? Do you feel any of them could have been avoided?
- What were some personal differences that tested your relationship? That strengthened it?
- How have differences in family backgrounds affected your marriage?
- How did you arrive at the decision that this was the right person? The right time?

- How or when did you first begin to experience doubts or misgivings about your relationship, and/or realize the honeymoon was over?
- As you look back, what might you have done to better prepare yourself for marriage?

2. For participants to fill out, then discuss with their partner:

a. Rank in order from 1 through 15 the top fifteen qualities you would consider most important in a spouse. (As in real life, you may not be able to get everything on the list below that you might like.)

___athletic

___similar background/lifestyle

___shares my religious beliefs

___kind and considerate

___shares household tasks

___dresses well

___high moral standards

___tolerant and forgiving

___nice physical appearance

___communicates openly and honestly

___makes me feel important

___likes being with people

___gets along well with family/friends

___likes children

___traditional height patterns

___has similar goals in life

___fun to be with

___earns good money

___values a close family life

___dependable

___well educated

___not jealous or possessive

___honest and truthful

___open-minded

___cares about me

___not previously married/divorced

___adventuresome

___ability to be a good parent

___affectionate

___wise and intelligent

___even-tempered

___similar hobbies and interests

___a faithful partner

___not in a previous sexual relationship

b. The following are commonly held *romantic myths* about mate selection. Do you agree or disagree?

___Any doubts I have will be gone once I have found the partner meant for me.

___There is only one right person in the world meant for me.

___No one else can be of any help when it comes to deciding when, whether, or whom to marry.

___People marry for only one reason: because they have found true love.

___Since opposites attract, the more unlike our interests and personality traits, the better.

___People who sincerely promise to correct their bad habits after they get married almost always do so.

c. Where on each continuum do you see yourself with regard to the following traits? How does the person you are considering marrying see you?

aggressive——————assertive——————passive

cocky——————self-confident——————insecure

life of the party——————sociable——————withdrawn

dictator——————negotiator——————doormat

rigid——————flexible——————wishy-washy

insensitive——————concerned——————oversensitive

short-tempered——————self-controlled——————apathetic

perfectionist——————well organized——————disorganized

wasteful——————careful——————miserly

work-addicted——————diligent——————lazy

optimistic——————hopeful——————pessimistic

d. Check, then compare and discuss each of the following areas where you would see basic *similarities*, rather than significant *differences*, being preferable in a relationship:

___religious faith and practices

___cultural and family backgrounds

___general lifestyle preferences, standard of living

___hobby and recreational interests

___occupational and vocational goals

___values, convictions on moral issues

___political preferences

___conversational interests

___attitudes toward children and about parenting styles

___basic personality traits

Appendix E
Some Wedding Planning Ideas

1. Traditional elements in wedding ceremonies:

Pre-service music (seating of guests, family members)

Processional music (as minister, groom, attendants, and then the bride, enter)

Welcome and giving of bride ritual

Music and meditation

Vows, exchange of rings, and/or lighting of unity candle rituals

Pronouncing couple officially married, followed by kiss

Presentation of couple as husband and wife

Recessional

2. Two Sample Wedding Vows

a. Jane, will you take John to be your husband to live together in the covenant of marriage? And will you love him, nurture him, be loyal to him in sickness and in health, and forsaking all others, be faithful to him as long as you both shall live? *I will.*

John, will you take Jane to be your wife to live together in the covenant of marriage? Will you love her, nurture her, be loyal to her in sickness and in health, and forsaking all others, be faithful to her as long as you both shall live? *I will.*

Will all of you celebrating with Jane and John the joy of their marriage, and witnessing their promises, do all in your power to uphold these two persons in their covenant? If so, then answer: *We will.*

b. Stan, do you, with God as your witness, offer the gift of your life and your love, in sacred trust, to Susan to be her faithful husband? *I do.*

Susan, do you, with God as your witness, offer the gift of your life and your love, in sacred trust, to Stan to be his faithful wife? *I do.*

And now, to you both, do you covenant together under God, to continue to love, honor, and cherish each other, in joy and in sorrow, in poverty and in prosperity, in sickness and in health? And do you promise to be faithful to each other alone, as long as you both shall live? *We do.*

Because of the covenant you have made before God and these witnesses, and by the authority of Christ and his church, we pronounce you husband and wife, in the name of the Father, and of the Son, and of the Holy Spirit. What God has joined together, let no one separate.

3. Some Innovative Wedding Ideas

• Have the wedding held as a part of a congregation's weekly worship service, with every member participating and adding their blessings.

• The groom and bride each enter with their respective parents, then symbolically "leave father and mother" and join each other at the front of the church.

• Each guest or guest family has a picture taken as he or she arrives, then fills out a three-by-five card with name and with words of blessing—all of which goes into a memory book for the couple.

• Instead of only the bride being "given away," the minister asks, "Who gives this man and this woman in marriage?" Each set of parents responds with "We do."

• Bride and groom wash each other's feet in the service as a sign of their commitment to serve each other.

• Blessings for the couple are read by parents, grandparents, and/or friends and other family members.

• Guests provide food for the reception in the form of a potluck meal, or the congregation provides the reception dinner as a way of showing their support for a member of the congregation being married.

• If the wedding is held outdoors or in a setting in which chairs are used for seating, have guests seated in the round or in a semicircle surrounding the couple.

• For a summer wedding, have guests bring flower arrangements for the wedding and/or reception.

• Have a PowerPoint slide show of the bride's and groom's growing-up years shown before the service, accompanied by the couple's favorite music.

• The bride and groom present a single rose to each set of parents before the ceremony.

• After the ceremony, the bride and groom serve as ushers, standing at the end of each pew (or row of chairs) to greet and thank guests as they leave for the reception.

• For an evening wedding, give each guest a single candle (protected by a drip catcher), and at the end of the ceremony have lights turned off except for a single candle at the front, which the bride and groom use to light their candle. The couple then takes this candle to the end of each aisle and has each guest light the person's candle next to them. This can be done in complete silence or with appropriate music in the background.

Appendix F
Jesus' Teachings About Money in the Sermon on the Mount

- We recognize our own spiritual poverty and our utter dependence on God (Matthew 5:3).

- We live a modest and humble life (5:5).

- We eagerly long for more of God's righteousness and justice for all (5:6).

- We show mercy toward those who are oppressed and in need (5:7).

- We are loving and generous even toward those who take advantage of us (5:38-42).

- We do not do our acts of charity to be praised by others (6:1-4).

- We pray that God's rule will prevail everywhere and that all God's children will have their needs met every day (6:9-11).

• We invest in God's eternity-based economy by giving to those in need (see Luke 12:33; 18:22) rather than storing up wealth we can't take with us (Matthew 6:19-23).

• We despise materialism (Mammon) and offer our single-minded love and loyalty to God (6:22-24).

• Like the "birds of the air," we refuse to worry about having enough to eat or wear, trusting that if we, like the birds, do our part, God will provide (6:25-27).

• We see ourselves as much more beautiful and valuable in God's eyes than the "lilies of the field" and so are not compelled to buy more things to make us more attractive or deserving (6:28-32).

• We seek to live under God's rule and standards of what it right and just, trusting God to provide for our basic needs (6:33-34).

Appendix G
Identifying Four Problem and Responsibility Areas

For each of the items below, indicate in which of the following categories you see each belonging: PFA (Problem Free Area), PPA (Personal Problem Area), SPA (Spouse's Problem Area), MPA (Mutual Problem Area). Discuss your answers with your partner.

Note: The same general issue (work or employment, for example) may include elements that belong to more than one problem area. Key questions to ask in determining what part of a given issue belongs where are (1) who is bothered by this? (neither, of course, if it's in the PFA), and (2) who has the *ability,* and therefore the *responsibility,* to handle this?

_________1. You enjoy a good walk with your spouse while you share some of your dreams for your future.

_________2. You would like to pay off the mortgage faster. Your spouse wants to save more for the children's college fund.

_________3. Your spouse gets a promotion with a nice raise, which really helps the family's finances.

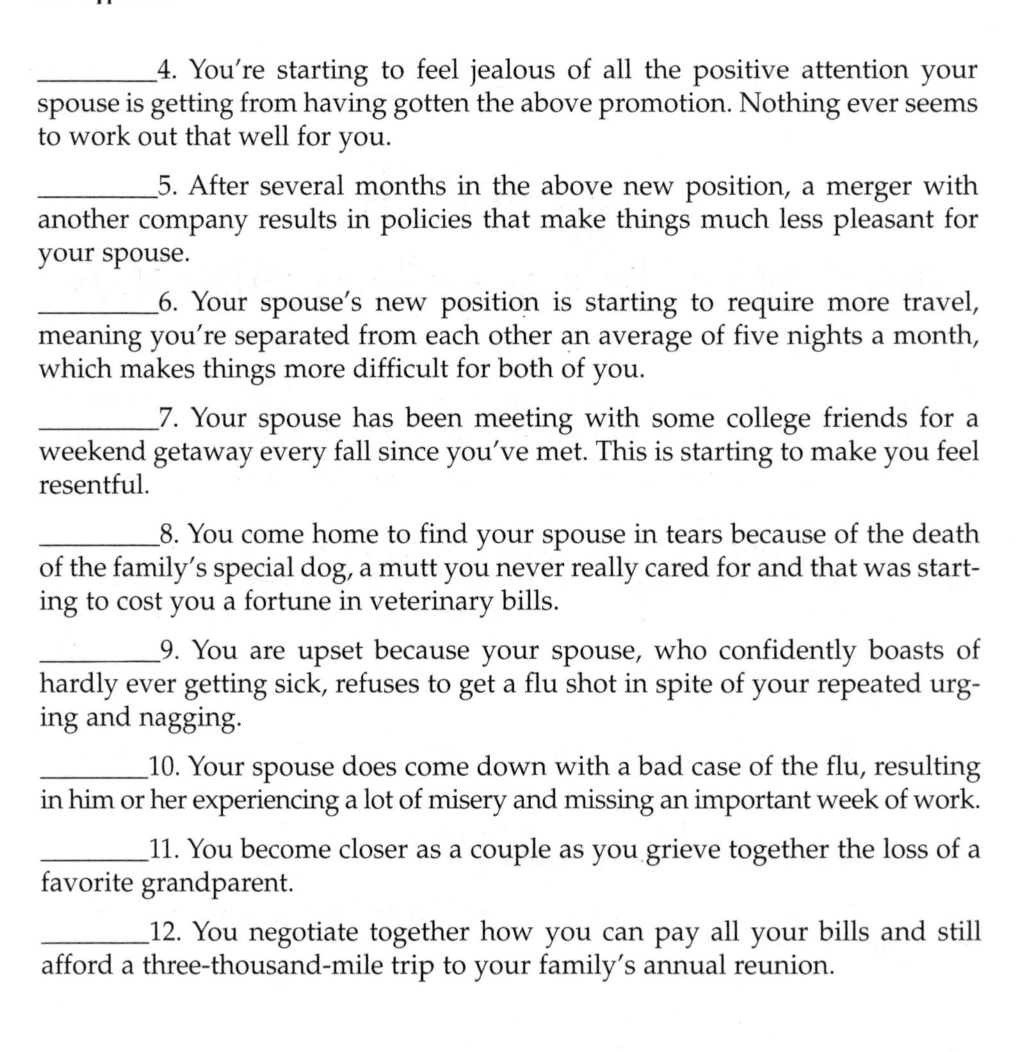

_________4. You're starting to feel jealous of all the positive attention your spouse is getting from having gotten the above promotion. Nothing ever seems to work out that well for you.

_________5. After several months in the above new position, a merger with another company results in policies that make things much less pleasant for your spouse.

_________6. Your spouse's new position is starting to require more travel, meaning you're separated from each other an average of five nights a month, which makes things more difficult for both of you.

_________7. Your spouse has been meeting with some college friends for a weekend getaway every fall since you've met. This is starting to make you feel resentful.

_________8. You come home to find your spouse in tears because of the death of the family's special dog, a mutt you never really cared for and that was starting to cost you a fortune in veterinary bills.

_________9. You are upset because your spouse, who confidently boasts of hardly ever getting sick, refuses to get a flu shot in spite of your repeated urging and nagging.

________10. Your spouse does come down with a bad case of the flu, resulting in him or her experiencing a lot of misery and missing an important week of work.

________11. You become closer as a couple as you grieve together the loss of a favorite grandparent.

________12. You negotiate together how you can pay all your bills and still afford a three-thousand-mile trip to your family's annual reunion.

________13. The two of you enjoy a week of vacation helping rebuild homes destroyed by a recent hurricane.

Answers: (1) PFA; (2) MPA; (3) PFA; (4) PPA; (5) SPA; (6) MPA; (7) PPA; (8) SPA; (9) PPA; (10) SPA; (11) MPA (& PFA?); (12) MPA; (13) PFA

Appendix H
Agape Love Inventory

Evaluate yourself on a scale of 0 to 5, with 0 being *not at all like me* and 5 being *like me most of the time* for each of the traits listed. Share your answers with your fiancé or your spouse and at least one good mentor or accountability partner. Then have someone you trust rate you on the following qualities associated with God's kind of tough and tender love (based on 1 Corinthians 13:4-8):

Love is patient.

___I am patient and persevering, not quick to give up on something or someone, especially not on my partner.

Love is kind.

___I try to show the same courtesy and care to my spouse as I want shown to myself.

Love is never jealous.

___I am not self-pitying or envious of my marriage partner (putting myself in an inferior position).

It never boasts, is never proud.

___I am not arrogant (putting myself in a superior position).

It does not act with rudeness

___I show a consistent courtesy and respect for both myself and my spouse.

. . . or insist on its rights.

___I am not overly concerned about proving I am right or about trying to get my own way.

It is not easily provoked.

___I am not oversensitive to my partner's slights or faults; I try not to take them too personally.

It keeps no record of wrongs.

___My mental bookkeeping is not weighted on the debit side.

Love is never glad when wrong is done

___I get no satisfaction from another's failure.

but is always glad when truth prevails.

___I look for, and affirm, any sign of improvement or progress in others.

It bears up under anything.

___My love is powerfully patient.

It exercises faith in everything.

___My love is powerfully confident.

It keeps up hope in everything.

___My love is powerfully positive.

It gives us power to endure in anything.

___My love is powerfully persevering.

Love never fails.

PFA
PPA
SPA
MPA

Appendix I
Agenda for Regular Couple's Meetings

1. Share compliments and appreciations.

2. Review any unfinished business from past meeting(s).

3. Review calendar and do necessary scheduling, including planning a date for the two of you.

4. Discuss any financial or budget issues, take care of paying bills, and so on.

5. Agree on an agenda, then take one item or problem at a time, as follows:

   a. First discuss the issue in terms of each of your underlying interests (Why this is important?), rather than first stating your positions (This is what we should do).

   b. Throughout, always take turns being the speaker and the listener. When you are the listener, make sure you fully understand before you take your turn to speak.

   c. Take time to brainstorm ideas for possible solutions, generating as many new options as possible (no evaluating or critiquing during this part of the process).

d. After discussing some of the more agreeable options you now have on the table, decide by consensus. If you can't come up with a win-win solution, postpone the decision to a later time, agree on an interim solution, or see a mediator or counselor for help. Remember, no agreement needs to be set in stone for all time, but should be honored until it is reviewed and changed.

e. Decide how and by whom a decision is to be carried out and what will happen if it isn't. To avoid misunderstandings, put both the agreement and any friendly, agreed-on consequence (for not following through) in writing.

6. Decide on a time for your next couple's meeting and on who will be responsible for making sure the session happens. Of course, either partner can respectfully ask for a special session at any time it is agreeable to the other.

7. Keep it under an hour, and end with some activity you both enjoy.

Appendix J
Things to Look for in a Marriage Counselor

• The therapist has earned a good reputation for trustworthiness and confidentiality.

• She or he is "marriage friendly," affirming the belief that existing relationships are better salvaged whenever possible.

• You both feel comfortable and safe with the person you choose (some counselors offer a free initial consultation to get acquainted and to discuss options).

• The counselor doesn't allow verbal conflicts to escalate in sessions, but sets clear boundaries and gives directions for constructive ways of interacting.

• He or she focuses on your strengths—and on the good reasons you chose each other in the first place—and helps you rebuild your relationship on the basis of those strengths.

• The counselor suggests assignments to do between appointments, using the sessions as "huddles" in which the two of you (the team members), meet with your chosen coach for direction and encouragement in practicing new behaviors where the real changes need to be made—at home.

• Your counselor is willing to refer elsewhere if necessary—for individual counseling, for a more intensive marital recovery program, or to another therapist—if no progress is made after a reasonable time.

Ed, intent on splitting with his wife, decides to place a personal ad.

Appendix K
A Prenuptial Covenant for Couples

Identify and discuss each of your positions on the following:[18]

1. Family Faith
   a. Church membership
   b. Church attendance
   c. Bible reading and prayer (daily? individually? as a couple? as a family?)
2. Household chores (how divided or shared?)
3. Children
   a. How many?
   b. When and how far apart?
   c. General approach to discipline
   d. What if we can't have children?
   e. What if we have unplanned children?
4. Work
   a. Both work outside the home?
   b. What career goals?
5. Money
   a. Expected or hoped-for income
   b. Saving and spending
   c. Will we go into debt? For what items?
   d. Who does bookkeeping?
   e. How much giving to church/ charity?

f. How much is each free to spend without consulting the other?

6. Privacy rights
   a. Opening and reading each other's mail or e-mail?
   b. Allowing each other alone time and space?

7. Social needs
   a. Regular and special times together? How often?
   b. Individual times for friends or personal interests
   c. Regular vacations?
   d. Common interests or hobbies?

8. Parents
   a. Frequency of visits with each set of parents
   b. Accept loans or gifts from parents?

9. Communication
   a. Regular dates together?
   b. Regular "couple's meetings" to review schedules and finances, and to work on any problems in the relationship?

10. Sex
    a. Complete fidelity in all respects!
    b. What method of birth control?
    c. Times to share freely our needs and feelings about this part of our relationship?

11. Seeking help
    a. We agree to meet with a counselor six months after our marriage to review how our relationship is progressing.
    b. We covenant to seek pastoral or professional help if we have any difficulty we are unable to resolve between us.

Covenanters: ______________________ ______________________

Date ____________

Appendix L

Summary of Homework Ideas for the Four Problem Areas

Problem-Free Area

Write frequent love notes, give hugs and back rubs regularly.

Have regular couple's meetings.

Enjoy at-home "mini-dates" on a regular basis.

Read something inspirational and/or pray together daily.

Develop traditions around special events and anniversaries.

Take in a marriage seminar or retreat.

Practice making at least four positive comments for each statement about a problem or concern.

Share household chores.

Personal Problem Area

Take a fearless inventory of your own faults and areas where you need to grow.

Invite your partner to suggest areas of growth for your life.

Choose a mentor, pastor, counselor, or spiritual director to help you work on changes you want to make.

Mentally rehearse new behaviors and ways of responding, and practice them regularly.

Keep a journal of your growth goals and of notes on your progress.

Spouse's Problem Area

Practice deep and patient listening.

Practice stating concerns you have about your partner less frequently and as a wish—or as a part of an "I message."

Show active support and encouragement.

Pray for your partner every day.

Practice showing unconditional acceptance of your partner (doesn't mean you approve of all his or her behaviors).

Mutual Problem Area

Have a couple's meeting once a week.

Ask permission before bringing up a problem for discussion at other times.

Start each meeting with a time of simply discussing an issue (and generating ideas) before working at deciding anything.

Take turns being the speaker and the listener.

Keep notes of significant actions or decisions.

Agree on a means of accountability for making sure agreements are kept.

Get outside help if necessary.

Notes

1. David W. Augsburger, *Sustaining Love* (Ventura, CA: Regal Press, 1988), p. 55.

2. Copyright © 2001. All rights reserved. Used by permission.

3. Robert T. Michael, et al., *Sex in America: A Definitive Survey* (Little, Brown and Company, 1995) p. 112.

4. Clifford Notarious and Howard Markman, *We Can Work It Out* (New York: G. P. Putnam's Sons, 1993), p. 39.

5. Adapted with permission from material in Philip Osborne's book, *Parenting for the '90s* (Intercourse, PA: Good Books, 1989), pp. 14-22.

6. Katherine Greider and Roberta Yared, *AARP Bulletin*, March 2006, "Lovemaking: Dump the TV" p. 36.

7. Rabbi Joseph Telushkin, *Words That Hurt, Words That Heal: How to Choose Words Wisely and Well* (New York: Wm. Morrow and Co., 1996), p. xvii.

8. Glenn T. Stanton, *1998 South Carolina Marital Health Study* (Palmetto Family Council, 1998), p. 32.

9. Tom Sine, *The Mustard Seed Conspiracy* (Waco, TX: Word Books, 1981), p. 158.

10. Elliott Merrick, *Green Mountain Farm* (New York: Macmillan, 1948), p. 80.

11. Barbara H. Fiese, et al., *American Psychological Association Journal of Family Psychology*, December 2002, "A Review of 50 Years of Research on Naturally Occurring Family Routines and Rituals: Cause for Celebration?" p. 385 ff.

12. David Kline, *Great Possessions: An Amish Farmer's Journal* (San Francisco: North Point Press, 1990), p. xxiii.

13. Luann Austin, "Family Meals Beget a Healthy Family Life," *Daily News-Record* (Harrisonburg, Virginia), September 5, 2003, p. 13.

14. David Wilcox, from "Covert War" © 1991 Universal Music Publishing.

15. Carol Travis, *Anger, the Misunderstood Emotion* (New York: Simon and Schuster, 1982), p. 41.

16. Telushkin, *Words That Hurt, Words That Heal*, p. 72.

17. Cyril A. and Renee Travis Reilly, *An Irish Blessing: A Photographic Interpretation* (Notre Dame, IN: Sorin Books, 1999).

18. Adapted with permission from John M. Drescher from unpublished material.

The Author

Harvey Yoder is a licensed counselor and marital therapist at Family Life Resource Center in Harrisonburg, Virginia, where he also teaches parenting classes and offers workshops on mental health and relationship issues. He serves as pastoral leader of Family of Hope, a Mennonite house church congregation. He holds graduate degrees from James Madison University and Eastern Mennonite Seminary. He was born in Watova, Oklahoma, to an Amish family. He worked for many years as a teacher and pastor, and he has written numerous articles on marriage, family, and other relationships.

The Illustrator

Lee Eshleman is a partner in the performance duo Ted & Lee, whose original comedy-theater has enlivened the biblical story since 1987. Lee's illustrations have appeared in numerous publications and electronic media, including *HealthCare, Flying Disc,* Mennonite Media's "Third Way" web site, *The Little Book on Trauma,* and *Without the Loss of One*. He was born in Richmond and now lives in Harrisonburg, Virginia.

UNLIMITED LIFETIME WARRANTY

With God as our shepherd . . .

we will not be in want

we will experience abundant peace

our inner beings will be restored

we will be led in the right path

we need not fear going through the darkest of valleys

God will . . .

provide protection and guidance

prepare a peace table for us

anoint our heads with healing oil

fill our lives to overflowing

Surely goodness and mercy will follow us all the days of our lives, and we will live in God's house of blessing forever.

—Based on Psalm 23